FIFTH EDITION

Focus on
Grammar 3

WORKBOOK

Marjorie Fuchs

Focus on Grammar 3: An Integrated Skills Approach, Fifth Edition Workbook

Pearson Education, Inc., 221 River Street, Hoboken, NJ 07030

Staff credits: The people who made up the *Focus on Grammar 3, Fifth Edition Workbook* team, representing content creation, design, manufacturing, marketing, multimedia, project management, publishing, rights management, and testing, are Pietro Alongi, Rhea Banker, Elizabeth Barker, Stephanie Bullard, Jennifer Castro, Tracey Cataldo, Aerin Csigay, Mindy DePalma, Warren Fischbach, Pam Fishman, Nancy Flaggman, Lester Holmes, Malgorzata Hordecka, Gosia Jaros-White, Leslie Johnson, Barry Katzen, Amy McCormick, Julie Molnar, Brian Panker, Stuart Radcliffe, Lindsay Richman, Alexandra Suarez, Paula Van Ells, and Joseph Vella.

Text design and layout: Page Designs International
Composition: ElectraGraphics, Inc.
Contributing editor: Lise Minovitz

Cover image: Andy Roberts/Getty Images
Photo credits: Page 3 (bottom): Ints Vikmanis/Fotolia; 3 (top): Ints Vikmanis/Fotolia; 5 (left): Michaeljung/Fotolia; 5 (right): Luismolinero/Fotolia; 8: Studio 8/Pearson Education, Ltd; 13 (bottom): Everett Collection Inc/Alamy Stock Photo; 13 (top): Everett Collection Historical/Alamy Stock Photo; 14: Pictorial Press Ltd/Alamy Stock Photo; 17: Sputnik/Alamy Stock Photo; 23: PA Photos/ABACA/Newscom; 50 (bottom): Corinne Dubreuil/ABACA/Newscom; 50 (top): Epa European Pressphoto Agency B.V./Alamy Stock Photo; 62: LightRocket/Getty Images; 064: Julia Dementeva/Shutterstock; 71: Mike Ledray/Shutterstock; 74: dpa picture alliance archive/Alamy Stock Photo; 75: Outdoorsman/Shutterstock; 86: Pictorial Press Ltd/Alamy; 105: Jose Ignacio Soto/Shutterstock; 106: Sculpies/Shutterstock; 113: Soru Epotok/Fotolia; 124: Maksym Bondarchuk/Shutterstock; 129: Raulcrego/Fotolia; 132: Boldg/Fotolia; 146: Shutterstock; 151: Bloomicon/Shutterstock; 151: Serg64/Shutterstock; 170: Vladimir Wrangel/Fotolia; 183: Boldg/Fotolia.
Illustrations: Steve Attoe: p. 2; ElectraGraphics, Inc.: pp. 3, 35, 63, 91, 96-97, 101, 112, 135-136, 140, 157, 173, 175-176; Susan Scott: pp. 26, 192, 194

ISBN 10: 0-13-457959-3
ISBN 13: 978-0-13-457959-7

Printed in the United States of America
  9 2019

Contents

About the Author

Marjorie Fuchs has taught ESL at New York City Technical College and LaGuardia Community College of the City University of New York and EFL at Sprachstudio Lingua Nova in Munich, Germany. She has a master's degree in Applied English Linguistics and a certificate in TESOL from the University of Wisconsin–Madison. She has authored and co-authored many widely used books and multimedia materials, notably *Crossroads 4*; *Top Twenty ESL Word Games: Beginning Vocabulary Development*; *Families: Ten Card Games for Language Learners*; *Focus on Grammar 3* and *4* (editions 1–5); *Focus on Grammar 3* and *4, CD-ROM*; *Longman English Interactive 3* and *4*; *Grammar Express Basic*; *Grammar Express Basic CD-ROM*; *Grammar Express Intermediate*; *Future 1: English for Results*; *OPD Workplace Skills Builder*; and workbooks for *Crossroads 1–4*; *The Oxford Picture Dictionary High Beginning* and *Low Intermediate*, (editions 1–3); *Focus on Grammar 3* and *4* (editions 1–5); and *Grammar Express Basic*.

Present Progressive and Simple Present

EXERCISE 1 SPELLING

Write the correct forms of the verbs. Make spelling changes where necessary.

	-ing	-s or -es
1. begin	*beginning*	*begins*
2. come		
3. do		
4. get		
5. go		
6. have		
7. live		
8. look		
9. meet		
10. plan		
11. play		
12. read		
13. run		
14. say		
15. start		
16. study		
17. take		
18. watch		
19. work		
20. write		

EXERCISE 2 PRESENT PROGRESSIVE OR SIMPLE PRESENT

Complete the paragraphs with the correct form of the verbs in parentheses. Choose between affirmative and negative. Use information from the cartoons. Use contractions when possible.

It's 6:10. Amy _____ *has* _____ a 6:00 appointment with Dan at Café Blue. Dan
        1. (have)

_____ to the café. He _____ a watch, and he _____ like
        2. (walk)   **3.** (wear)   **4.** (look)

he is in a hurry.

Amy _____ Dan, but she _____ his behavior. Why _____
        5. (like)   **6.** (understand)   **7.** (be)

he always late? She _____ at the café clock, and she _____ annoyed.
                    8. (look)   **9.** (get)

Amy _____ Dan's behavior _____ bad. But maybe it's just a
        10. (think)   **11.** (be)

cross-cultural misunderstanding. After all, Amy and Dan _____ from two different
                                                        12. (come)

countries, and people from different cultures often _____ in different ways.
                                                    13. (act)

EXERCISE 3 PRESENT PROGRESSIVE OR SIMPLE PRESENT

Complete the postcards with the present progressive or simple present form of the verbs from the boxes. Use contractions when possible.

| get | have | look | rain | stand | start | take | ~~travel~~ |

A.

Dear Carlos,

I really love living abroad. We do a lot of traveling because the distance between countries isn't that big. Right now, Ana and I _____are traveling_____ through England. At the moment, I _____ in front of
  1.   **2.**
Big Ben. It's a cloudy day. The sky _____ darker by the minute. It
                                                  3.
_____ like it's going to rain. (It _____ here a lot!) Ana
  4.   **5.**
_____ her camera, and she _____ pictures. I've got to run! It
  6.   **7.**
_____ to rain.
  8.
See you in a few weeks!

Marcos

| help | improve | live | love | mean | miss | speak | study | want |

B.

Dear Amanda,

Here I am in Paris! I _____ it here. It's a beautiful
                              1.
city. I _____ French and _____ with a
            2.   **3.**
French family—the Michauds. My French _____ because I
                                                4.
always _____ it "at home." I'm happy. This is a good thing because
            5.
it _____ there are fewer misunderstandings!
      6.
The Michauds are great. They _____ me find a job. I
                                        7.
_____ to save enough money to travel in August. Why don't
  8.
you come and visit me? I _____ you!
                                  9.
Melissa

EXERCISE 4 AFFIRMATIVE STATEMENTS

Aldo and Emilia Bottero are students. Look at what they do every day. Complete the sentences about their activities. Choose between the present progressive and the simple present.

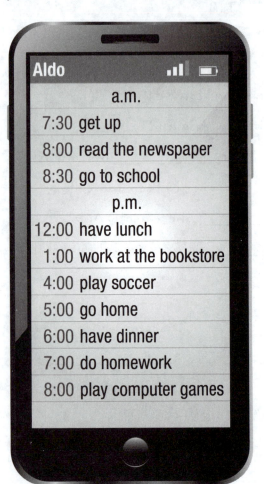

Aldo

a.m.

7:30	get up
8:00	read the newspaper
8:30	go to school

p.m.

12:00	have lunch
1:00	work at the bookstore
4:00	play soccer
5:00	go home
6:00	have dinner
7:00	do homework
8:00	play computer games

Emilia

a.m.

7:30	get up
8:00	run
8:30	go to school

p.m.

12:00	have lunch
1:00	study at the library
4:00	play basketball
5:00	do homework at the library
6:00	practice the guitar
7:00	have dinner
8:00	watch TV

1. At 7:30 a.m., _Aldo and Emilia get up._

2. It's 8:00 a.m. _Aldo is reading the newspaper. Emilia is running._

3. At 8:30 a.m., _____

4. It's noon. _____

5. At 1:00 p.m., _____

6. At 4:00 p.m., _____

7. It's 5:00 p.m. _____

8. At 6:00 p.m., _____

9. At 7:00 p.m., _____

10. It's 8:00 p.m. _____

EXERCISE 5 AFFIRMATIVE AND NEGATIVE STATEMENTS

Read the article about Aldo and Emilia from the school newsletter. There are five mistakes in facts about their schedules. Look at their schedules in Exercise 4. Then correct the mistakes.

Modern Language Institute Newsletter

Welcome, New Students!

We are happy to welcome two new students, Aldo and Emilia Bottero from Rome, Italy. The Botteros have very busy schedules. They both get up at 8:30 every morning. Then Aldo watches TV, and Emilia goes for her morning run. They then leave for the Institute where they are studying English and American culture this summer. At noon, they have lunch together.

After lunch, Emilia works at the bookstore. Both students love all types of sports. These days Aldo is playing soccer and Emilia is playing tennis. Emilia also plays the guitar. "Living abroad is a great experience, and we're very happy to be here," they said. Their days are busy, but they always have dinner together—just like back home in Italy.

---

1. *They don't get up at 8:30.*

   They get up at 7:30.

2. _____

   _____

3. _____

   _____

4. _____

   _____

5. _____

   _____

EXERCISE 6 QUESTIONS AND SHORT ANSWERS

Use the words in parentheses and the present progressive or simple present to write questions about Aldo and Emilia. Look at their schedules in Exercise 4 and answer the questions.

1. (Aldo and Emilia / go to school)

A: _Do Aldo and Emilia go to school?_ _____

B: _Yes, they do._ _____

2. (When / Aldo and Emilia / get up)

A: _____

B: _____

3. (Emilia / walk in the morning)

A: _____

B: _____

4. It's 12:00. (What / they / do now)

A: _____

B: _____

5. It's 1:00. (Aldo / do homework now)

A: _____

B: _____

6. (Emilia / do her homework at school)

A: _____

B: _____

7. (When / Emilia / play basketball)

A: _____

B: _____

8. (Aldo / play computer games before dinner)

A: _____

B: _____

EXERCISE 7 ADVERBS AND WORD ORDER

Unscramble the words to make sentences. Use the correct form of the verbs in parentheses.

1. Aldo / the newspaper / (read) / always

   Aldo always reads the newspaper.

2. on time / usually / Emilia / (be)

   _____

3. never / school / Aldo and Emilia / (miss)

   _____

4. these days / they / (study) / English

   _____

5. usually / they / Italian / (speak)

   _____

6. (speak) / English / now / they

   _____

7. (do) / their homework / Aldo and Emilia / always

   _____

8. (be) / Aldo / tired / often

   _____

9. usually / (eat) / the students / in school / lunch

   _____

10. hungry / they / (be) / always

    _____

11. Emilia / at the moment / (have) / a snack

    _____

12. (go) / to bed / rarely / Emilia / late

    _____

EXERCISE 8 EDITING

Read the student's email. There are eleven mistakes in the use of the present progressive or simple present. The first mistake is already corrected. Find and correct ten more.

Hi Andrew!

How are you? ~~I write~~ *I'm writing* you this email before my class.

I'm having a part-time job as a clerk in the mailroom of a small company. The pay isn't good, but I'm liking the people there. They're all friendly, and we are speaking Spanish all the time. I'm also taking classes at night school. I'm studying the language and culture of this country. The class is meeting three times a week. It just started last week, so I'm not knowing many of the other students yet. They seem nice, though.

I'm thinking that I'm beginning to get accustomed to living here. At first, I experienced some "culture shock." I understand that this is quite normal. But these days I meet more and more people because of my job and my class, so I'm feeling more connected to things. I'm also having fewer misunderstandings because of the language.

What do you do these days? Do you still look for a new job?

Please write when you can. I'm always liking to hear from you.

Brian

EXERCISE 9 PERSONAL WRITING

Write one or two paragraphs about your life these days. Are you busy? Are you relaxed?
Use the present progressive and the simple present. Use some of the phrases from
the box.

I always	I sometimes
At the moment, I	Right now
Every morning	These days

EXAMPLE: My life is very busy these days. I'm working on an important project at my job.
Every morning, I . . .

_____

_____

_____

_____

_____

_____

_____

_____

_____

_____

2 Simple Past

EXERCISE 1 SPELLING: REGULAR AND IRREGULAR VERBS

Write the simple past form of the verbs.

	Base Form	Simple Past			Base Form	Simple Past
1.	answer	*answered*		16.	look	_____
2.	begin	_____		17.	meet	_____
3.	buy	_____		18.	move	_____
4.	catch	_____		19.	need	_____
5.	come	_____		20.	open	_____
6.	die	_____		21.	put	_____
7.	do	_____		22.	read	_____
8.	feel	_____		23.	say	_____
9.	find	_____		24.	see	_____
10.	get	_____		25.	take	_____
11.	give	_____		26.	think	_____
12.	have	_____		27.	understand	_____
13.	hurry	_____		28.	vote	_____
14.	kiss	_____		29.	win	_____
15.	live	_____		30.	write	_____

31. The past of *be* is _____   _____

EXERCISE 2 AFFIRMATIVE AND NEGATIVE STATEMENTS: *BE*

Look at the chart of famous writers of the past. Complete the sentences with *was, wasn't, were,* and *weren't.*

ISAAK BABEL	1894–1940	Russia	short-story writer, playwright[1]
SIMONE DE BEAUVOIR	1908–1986	France	novelist,[2] essayist[3]
KAREL ČAPEK	1890–1938	Czechoslovakia	novelist, essayist
AGATHA CHRISTIE	1890–1976	England	mystery writer
LORRAINE HANSBERRY	1930–1965	United States	playwright
NÂZIM HIKMET	1902–1963	Turkey	poet, playwright, novelist
LUCY M. MONTGOMERY	1874–1942	Canada	poet, novelist
PABLO NERUDA	1904–1973	Chile	poet
WANG WEI	701–761	China	poet, musician, painter

[1] *playwright:* a person who writes plays
[2] *novelist:* a person who writes novels (books that are fiction)
[3] *essayist:* a person who writes essays (short pieces of writing about a topic)

1. Simone de Beauvoir _____ wasn't _____ a French poet.

   She _____ was _____ a French novelist.

2. Wang Wei _____ born in 699.

3. Lucy M. Montgomery and Lorraine Hansberry _____ South American writers.

   They _____ North American writers.

4. Karel Čapek _____ a poet.

5. Pablo Neruda _____ from Chile.

6. Agatha Christie _____ American.

   She _____ British.

7. Isaak Babel _____ Russian.

   He _____ French.

8. Nâzim Hikmet _____ from Russia.

   He _____ from Turkey.

9. Babel and Hikmet _____ both playwrights.

10. Pablo Neruda and Simone de Beauvoir _____ both born in the early 1900s.

EXERCISE 3 QUESTIONS AND ANSWERS WITH THE PAST OF *BE*

Use *was* and *wasn't* and the words in parentheses to write questions about the people in Exercise 2. Look at the chart in Exercise 2 and answer the questions.

1. (Lorraine Hansberry / a playwright)

   A: _Was Lorraine Hansberry a playwright?_

   B: _Yes, she was._

2. (Where / Simone de Beauvoir from)

   A: _____

   B: _____

3. (What nationality / Pablo Neruda)

   A: _____

   B: _____

4. (Who / Wang Wei)

   A: _____

   B: _____

5. (Agatha Christie / French)

   A: _____

   B: _____

6. (What nationality / Lucy M. Montgomery)

   A: _____

   B: _____

7. (Nâzim Hikmet / a poet)

   A: _____

   B: _____

8. (When / Karel Čapek / born)

   A: _____

   B: _____

EXERCISE 4 AFFIRMATIVE STATEMENTS

Complete the following short biographies with the simple past form of the verbs from the boxes.

~~be~~	begin	die	grow up	love	move	teach	use	write

A.

Béla Bartók (1881–1945) _____was_____ one of the most famous
1.

composers of the 20th century. Born in Hungary, he _____
2.

in a musical family. His mother _____ him how to play the
3.

piano, and at the age of nine, he _____ to write music.
4.

Bartók _____ the folk music of his native country. He
5.

_____ these folk tunes and folk music from other Eastern
6.

European countries in his own work. In addition to his compositions for musical instruments, he also

_____ an opera and a ballet. Bartók _____ to the United States in 1940
7.   **8.**

and _____ there at the age of 64.
9.

be	begin	die	have	love	marry	paint	plan	study	teach

B.

Frida Kahlo (1907–1954) _____ one of the most famous
1.

Mexican painters. At first, she _____ to be a doctor, but after a
2.

serious accident she _____ painting from her bed. Her topics
3.

were her family and friends. She also _____ many pictures
4.

of herself. Kahlo never _____ art in school. She
5.

_____ herself how to paint. People _____ her
6.   **7.**

work, and she had many admirers. In 1929, she _____ Diego Rivera, another very
8.

famous Mexican painter. Unfortunately, Kahlo _____ a lot of serious medical
9.

problems, and she _____ at the age of 47.
10.

(continued on next page)

| be | build | fly | go | last | take place | watch |

C.

Orville Wright (1871–1948) and **Wilbur Wright** (1867–1912)

_____ American airplane inventors. The two brothers
1.

_____ to high school, but they never graduated. They
2.

_____ their first planes in their bicycle shop in Ohio. On
3.

December 17, 1903, Orville _____ their plane, *Flyer 1,* for the
4.

first time. It was a short journey—just a distance of 120 feet (37 meters).

Wilbur, four other men, and a boy _____ from the ground below. This first controlled,
5.

power-driven flight _____ near Kitty Hawk, North Carolina. It _____
6.   7.

only about 12 seconds.

EXERCISE 5 QUESTIONS AND ANSWERS

Use the words in parentheses and the simple past to write questions about the people in
Exercise 4. Look at the information in Exercise 4 and answer the questions.

Biography A

1. (When / Béla Bartók / live)

   A: *When did Béla Bartók live?*

   B: *He lived from 1881 to 1945.*

2. (Where / he / grow up)

   A: _____

   B: _____

3. (What / he / do)

   A: _____

   B: _____

4. (he / spend / his whole life in Hungary)

   A: _____

   B: _____

5. (Frida Kahlo / plan to be a painter)

A: _____

B: _____

6. (When / she / begin painting)

A: _____

B: _____

7. (What / she / paint)

A: _____

B: _____

8. (When / she / die)

A: _____

B: _____

Biography C

9. (Where / the Wright brothers / build their first planes)

A: _____

B: _____

10. (both brothers / fly the *Flyer 1*)

A: _____

B: _____

11. (Where / the first controlled flight / take place)

A: _____

B: _____

12. (How long / the flight / last)

A: _____

B: _____

EXERCISE 6 NEGATIVE STATEMENTS

There were a lot of similarities between the Wright brothers, but there were also differences. Complete the chart about the differences between Orville and Wilbur.

Orville	Wilbur
1. Orville talked a lot.	*Wilbur didn't talk a lot.*
2. *Orville didn't spend a lot of time alone.*	Wilbur spent a lot of time alone.
3. _____	Wilbur had serious health problems.
4. Orville grew a mustache.	_____
5. _____	Wilbur lost most of his hair.
6. Orville took courses in Latin.	_____
7. Orville liked to play jokes.	_____
8. Orville dressed very fashionably.	_____
9. Orville played the guitar.	_____
10. _____	Wilbur built the first glider.
11. _____	Wilbur made the first attempts to fly.
12. _____	Wilbur chose the location of Kitty Hawk.
13. Orville had a lot of patience.	_____
14. Orville lived a long life.	_____

EXERCISE 7 EDITING

Read the student's short biography of a famous person. There are fourteen mistakes in the use of the simple past. The first mistake is already corrected. Find and correct thirteen more.

Pablo Neruda (1904–1973) ~~were~~ ^{was} a famous poet, political activist, and ambassador.[1] He was born in Parral, Chile. His mother, a school teacher, dies just two months after Neruda's birth. His father work for the railroad. He no support Neruda's early interest in writing. He wanted him to do something more "practical." When he was seventeen, Neruda gone to Santiago to continue his education. At first, he planned to become a teacher like his mother, but soon he beginned to write poems. He did not finished school, but he published his first book of poetry before he were twenty. In one of his love poems, he describe "restless rocks" at the bottom of the ocean. Like the rocks in his poem, Neruda did not stayed in one place. He spends decades traveling and writing poetry. His poems did show strong emotions and beautiful imagery.[2] In 1971, while he was Chile's ambassador to France, he winned the Nobel Prize in literature. Neruda dead two years later.

---

[1] **ambassador:** a person who officially represents his or her country in a foreign country
[2] **imagery:** the use of words to describe ideas or actions

EXERCISE 8 PERSONAL WRITING

Write a paragraph about your experience learning English. Answer the questions from the box.

> Where were you born?
> If you are now living in a different country, when did you come here?
> What language did you speak at home when you were a child?
> When did you begin to learn English?
> Where did you learn it?
> When did you start English classes here?

EXAMPLE: I was born in Mexico, but I moved here with my family five years ago. When I was a child, I spoke . . .

_____

_____

_____

_____

_____

_____

_____

_____

_____

UNIT 3 Past Progressive and Simple Past

EXERCISE 1 AFFIRMATIVE AND NEGATIVE STATEMENTS WITH THE PAST PROGRESSIVE

Frank Cotter is a financial manager. Read his schedule. Use the affirmative or negative past progressive to complete the sentences.

1. At 9:30, Mr. Cotter _____*was meeting*_____ with Ms. Jacobs.

2. At 9:30, he _____ financial reports.

3. At 11:30, he _____ correspondence.

4. At 12:30, he and Mr. Webb _____ lunch at Sol's Café.

5. They _____ at Frank's Diner.

6. At 3:30, he and Alan _____ sales reports.

7. They _____ the budget.

8. At 4:30, he _____ correspondence.

9. He _____ phone calls.

10. At 8:00, he _____ a lecture on the *Titanic*.

April 14	Wednesday
9:00–10:00	meet with Ms. Jacobs
10:00–11:00	write financial reports
11:00–12:00	answer correspondence[1]
12:00–1:00	eat lunch with Mr. Webb at Sol's Café
2:00–4:00	discuss budget[2] with Alan
4:00–5:00	return phone calls
7:00–9:00	attend *Titanic* lecture at City University

[1] *correspondence:* letters and emails
[2] *budget:* a plan on how to spend money

EXERCISE 2 QUESTIONS AND ANSWERS WITH THE PAST PROGRESSIVE

Use the words in parentheses to write questions. Look at the schedule in Exercise 1 and write the answers. Use the past progressive.

1. (Mr. Cotter / meet / with Mr. Webb at 9:30)

   A: *Was Mr. Cotter meeting with Mr. Webb at 9:30?*

   B: *No, he wasn't.*

(continued on next page)

2. (What / he / do at 9:30)

A: _____

B: _____

3. (Mr. Cotter / write police reports at 10:30)

A: _____

B: _____

4. (What kind of reports / he / write)

A: _____

B: _____

5. (What / he / do at 11:30)

A: _____

B: _____

6. (he / have lunch at 12:00)

A: _____

B: _____

7. (Who / eat lunch with him)

A: _____

B: _____

8. (Where / they / have lunch)

A: _____

B: _____

9. (Who / he / talk to at 3:30)

A: _____

B: _____

EXERCISE 3 STATEMENTS WITH THE PAST PROGRESSIVE AND SIMPLE PAST

Read the newspaper article. Complete the story with the past progressive or simple past form of the verbs in parentheses.

HIT AND RUN

NEW YORK, June 30—Last Friday at 9:30 p.m., a blue Honda Accord _____*hit*_____
1. (hit)

thirty-five-year-old Lisa Coleman while she _____ the street at Broadway and
2. (cross)

10th Avenue. Witnesses say that the car _____ and _____
3. (speed) **4. (not stop)**

at the red light.

Frank Cotter, a financial manager at Smith Webber, _____ on his way home
5. (be)

from a lecture when he _____ the accident. "I _____ along
6. (see) **7. (walk)**

Broadway when I _____ this blue Honda. I _____ it because
8. (see) **9. (notice)**

it _____ very fast. When it _____ the intersection, the driver
10. (go) **11. (reach)**

_____ right through the red light. Just seconds later, the blue Honda
12. (go)

_____ the pedestrian. I immediately _____ my cell phone
13. (hit) **14. (take out)**

and _____ the police. The driver _____."
15. (call) **16. (not stop)**

The accident _____ not far from the nearest hospital, and the ambulance
17. (happen)

_____ quickly. When it _____ to the scene of the accident,
18. (come) **19. (get)**

Coleman _____ on the ground. She _____ from a head
20. (lie) **21. (bleed)**

wound, but she _____ conscious and pretty calm, and two police officers
22. (be)

_____ her about the accident.
23. (question)

Coleman _____ that she _____ the street when the car
24. (say) **25. (cross)**

_____ through the light and _____ her down. "It all
26. (go) **27. (knock)**

_____ so quickly," she said. "I _____ a green light, and I
28. (happen) **29. (have)**

_____ the street when all of a sudden—boom! I _____ the car."
30. (cross) **31. (not see)**

Coleman _____ her arm and _____ some injuries to her
32. (break) **33. (have)**

head, but fortunately, they _____ very serious. Police are still looking for the
34. (not be)

driver of the Honda.

EXERCISE 4 QUESTIONS WITH THE PAST PROGRESSIVE AND SIMPLE PAST

The police are interviewing another witness to the accident. Use the words in parentheses and the past progressive or simple past to write the interview questions.

1. (What / you / do / when the accident / happen)

   OFFICER: _What were you doing when the accident happened?_

   WITNESS: I was riding my bike home from school when I heard a loud noise.

2. (What / you / do / when you / hear the noise)

   OFFICER: _____

   WITNESS: I got off my bike and looked in the direction of the sound.

3. (What / you / see / when you / look in the direction of the sound)

   OFFICER: _____

   WITNESS: I saw a car—a blue Honda.

4. (Where / you / stand / when you / see the Honda)

   OFFICER: _____

   WITNESS: I was at the corner of Broadway and 10th.

5. (the driver / stop / when the accident / occur)

   OFFICER: _____

   WITNESS: No. The driver didn't stop. He immediately left the area. It was terrible.

6. (What / happen / next)

   OFFICER: _____

   WITNESS: I tried to get the license plate number, but the car was moving too fast.

7. (you / get a look at the driver / while he / drive away)

   OFFICER: _____

   WITNESS: No, I didn't. I don't even know if it was a man or a woman.

8. (What / the victim / do / when the car / hit her)

   OFFICER: _____

   WITNESS: I don't know. I didn't see her before the car hit her.

EXERCISE 5 EDITING

Read the newspaper article from 2009. There are six mistakes in the use of the past progressive and simple past. The first mistake is already corrected. Find and correct five more.

Last *Titanic* Survivor Dead at Age 97

LONDON, June 31, 2009—Millvina Dean, the last survivor of the 1912 *Titanic* disaster, ~~was dying~~ *died* yesterday in Southampton, England. She was 97.

Dean had no memories of the disaster. She was only two months old when she and her family were passengers on the luxury ship's first voyage. The ship was sailing from Dean's hometown of Southampton, England, to New York City. On the night of April 14, they slept in their cabin when the ship hit a huge iceberg.

Dean's father became alarmed and immediately was sending his wife and two children to the lifeboats. Dean was believing her father's quick action saved their lives. Most people thought the ship was unsinkable. "My father didn't take a chance," she said.

Other passengers weren't as lucky. Just a few hours after the *Titanic* struck the iceberg, the ship was sinking to the bottom of the Atlantic. More than 1500 passengers and crew lost their lives, including Dean's father.

Dean's family returned to England, where she spent most of her long life. In her later years, she attended *Titanic* conferences and gave interviews. She moved into a nursing home when she was breaking her hip three years ago. Charles Haas, president of the Titanic International Society, said that with Dean's death, history lost "the last living link to the story" of the *Titanic*.

EXERCISE 6 PERSONAL WRITING

Write a paragraph about what you did yesterday evening. Use the simple past and the past progressive. Use some of the phrases from the box.

While I _____ home yesterday, I . . .
I _____ when I got home.
While I _____ dinner, I . . .
When I _____ dinner, I . . .
I _____ English when . . .
The phone _____ while I . . .

EXAMPLE: While I was walking home from school yesterday, I stopped and got a slice of pizza.
            When I finished eating, I took out my cell phone and called . . .

_____

_____

_____

_____

_____

_____

_____

_____

_____

UNIT 4 *Used to* and *Would*

EXERCISE 1 AFFIRMATIVE STATEMENTS WITH *USED TO*

Life in many countries isn't the way it used to be. Complete the sentences. Use *used to*.

1. In the past, _____*people used to ride*_____ horses.

   Now people ride in cars.

2. In the past, _____ by candlelight.

   Now people read by electric light.

3. In the past, _____ over open fires.

   Now people cook in microwave ovens.

4. In the past, _____ all of their clothes by hand.

   Now people wash most of their clothes in washing machines.

5. In the past, _____ manual typewriters.

   Now people use computers.

6. In the past, _____ many weeks to get a message to another country.

   Now it takes just a few seconds.

EXERCISE 2 AFFIRMATIVE AND NEGATIVE STATEMENTS WITH *USED TO*

Read the sentences about the assistant manager of a Florida bank, Mehmet Hassan. Complete the sentences with the correct affirmative or negative form of *used to* and the verbs in parentheses.

1. Mehmet _____*used to be*_____ a full-time student. Now he has a job at a bank.
                          (be)

2. He _____ stamps. Now he collects coins.
              (collect)

3. He _____ a car. Now he owns a 2016 Toyota Camry.
              (have)

4. Mehmet _____ the bus to work. Now he drives.
                        take)

5. The bus _____ crowded. These days it's hard to find a seat.
                      (be)

6. Mehmet _____ in Chicago. Then he moved to Miami.
                        (live)

(continued on next page)

7. He _____ Miami. Now he thinks it's a nice city.
(like)

8. He _____ a lot of people in Miami. Now he has a lot of friends there.
(know)

9. He _____ a lot of phone calls. Now he sends a lot of emails and texts instead.
(make)

10. He _____ to Chicago several times a year. These days he doesn't go there
(return)
very often.

EXERCISE 3 QUESTIONS AND ANSWERS WITH *USED TO*

Use *used to* and the words in parentheses to write questions about Lisa White. Look at the two ID cards to write the answers.

1. (live in California)

A: *Did she use to live in California?*

B: *No, she didn't.*

2. Lisa recently moved to Los Angeles. (Where / live)

A: _____

B: _____

3. Lisa lives in a house. (live in a house)

A: _____

B: _____

4. This is her first job. (What / do)

A: _____

B: _____

5. (Which school / attend)

A: _____

B: _____

6. Lisa looks very different from before. She has short hair. (have long hair)

A: _____

B: _____

7. (wear glasses)

A: _____

B: _____

8. Lisa's last name is different from before. (be married)

A: _____

B: _____

EXERCISE 4 *USED TO* OR *WOULD*

Complete the information about Lisa White with *used to* or *would* and the verbs in parentheses. Use *would* when possible.

Lisa White's life has changed a lot in the past few years. She ____*used to be*____ a student at
                1. (be)

City College in New York. Her days were very long. She _____ early every morning
                2. (get up)

and go to school. After class, she _____ to her part-time job at a pizza restaurant. She
        3. (go)

_____ home until 8:00, and then she _____ do her homework. Today,
4. (not get)   **5. (have to)**

Lisa has a 9–5 job at a bank, and her evenings and weekends are free.

Lisa is single now, but she _____ married. She got divorced last year before she
        6. (be)

moved to California. In New York, she and her husband lived in a small apartment. Lisa

_____ the city by bus or subway. Now she has a large house and she drives everywhere.
7. (get around)

It gives her a feeling of personal power. She _____ quite different, too. Today, Lisa has
        8. (look)

short hair, but as a student she always wore it long.

Lisa missed New York a lot when she first moved to L.A. She _____ back whenever
        9. (fly)

she had the chance. Now she is quite happy with her new life, although she still has a lot of good

memories of her old one.

EXERCISE 5 EDITING

Read the journal entry. There are eight mistakes in the use of *used to* and *would*. The first mistake is already corrected. Find and correct seven more.

Sunday, Oct. 5

Today, I ran into an old classmate. We used to ~~was~~ **be** in

the same science class. In fact, we would often study

together for tests. He was a very good student, and

he always would gets A's. At first, I almost didn't

recognize Jason! He looked so different. He would

have very dark hair. Now he's almost all gray. He also

used to being a little heavy. Now he's quite thin. And

he was wearing a suit and tie! I couldn't believe it.

He never use to dress that way. He only used to wore

jeans! His personality seemed different, too. He didn't

use to talk very much. People didn't dislike him, but

he wasn't very popular. In fact, I really would think

he was a little weird. Now he seems very outgoing. I

wonder what he thought of me! I'm sure I look and

act different from the way I was used to, too! I'm

really glad we ran into each other. We shared a lot

of the same memories. It was awesome! Maybe we'll

see each other again!

EXERCISE 6 PERSONAL WRITING

Write one or two paragraphs about how your life used to be different from the way it is now. Use some of the phrases from the box.

> When I was younger, I used to . . .
> Now, I . . .
> I would . . . for hours.
> My friends would . . .
> Sometimes I would . . .
> These days, I . . .; but when I was younger, I always used to . . .

EXAMPLE: When I was younger, I used to have a lot more free time than I have these days. I would spend hours with my friends. We would . . .

_____

_____

_____

_____

_____

_____

_____

_____

_____

Wh- Questions

EXERCISE 1 QUESTIONS ABOUT THE SUBJECT

Ask questions about the words in italics. Use *What, Whose, Who,* or *How many.*

1. *Something* happened last night.

   What happened last night?

2. *Someone's* phone rang at midnight.

   _____

3. *Someone* was calling for Michelle.

   _____

4. *Someone* was having a party.

   _____

5. *Some number of* people left the party.

   _____

6. *Something* surprised them.

   _____

7. *Someone's* friend called the police.

   _____

8. *Some number of* police arrived.

   _____

9. *Something* happened next.

   _____

10. *Someone* told the police about a theft.

    _____

11. *Someone's* jewelry disappeared.

    _____

12. *Some number of* necklaces vanished.

    _____

EXERCISE 2 QUESTIONS ABOUT THE OBJECT AND *WHY, WHEN,* OR *WHERE*

Use the cues to write questions about Megan Knight, an accountant in Texas. Then match the questions and answers.

Questions	Answers
e 1. Where / she / live?	**a.** Two years.
Where does she live?	
___ 2. How many rooms / her apartment / have?	**b.** By bus.
___ 3. How much rent / she / pay?	**c.** The first of the month.
___ 4. When / she / pay the rent?	**d.** Ling, Jackson, & Drew, Inc.
___ 5. Who / she / live with?	**e.** In Texas.
___ 6. What / she / do?	**f.** Five and a half.
___ 7. Which company / she / work for?	**g.** She's an accountant.
___ 8. How long / she / plan to stay there?	**h.** Her sister.
___ 9. How / she / get to work?	**i.** Because she doesn't like to drive.
___ 10. Why / she / take the bus?	**j.** About $800 a month.

EXERCISE 3 QUESTIONS ABOUT THE SUBJECT AND OBJECT AND *WHY, WHEN,* OR *WHERE*

Megan wrote a letter to her friend Janice. The letter got wet, and now Janice can't read some parts of it. What questions does Janice ask to get the missing information?

Dear Janice,

Hi! I just moved to ⸻ **1.** . I left Chicago because ⸻ **2.** .

⸻ **3.** moved with me, and we are sharing an apartment. I got a job in a ⸻ **4.** .

It started ⸻ **5.** .

The town people seem nice. Our apartment is great. It has ⸻ **6.** rooms. ⸻ **7.**

of the rooms come with carpeting, but two of them have beautiful wood floors. The rent isn't too

high either. We pay $ ⸻ **8.** a month.

We need to buy some ⸻ **9.** . ⸻ **10.** 's brother wants to visit her, so we really

need an extra bed.

By the way, ⸻ **11.** called last Sunday. I also spoke to ⸻ **12.** . They

want to visit us in ⸻ **13.** . Would you like to come? Is that a good time for you? Just for

the record, I want you to know that there's plenty of room because ⸻ **14.** .

Write and let me know.

Love,
Megan

---

1. *Where did you move?* ⸻

2. ⸻

3. ⸻

4. ⸻

5. ⸻

6. ⸻

7. ⸻

8. ⸻

9. ⸻

10. ⸻

11. _____

12. _____

13. _____

14. _____

EXERCISE 4 EDITING

Megan is on a jury. She took notes and made a list of questions. Read her questions. There are eight mistakes in the use of *wh-* questions. The first mistake is already corrected. Find and correct seven more.

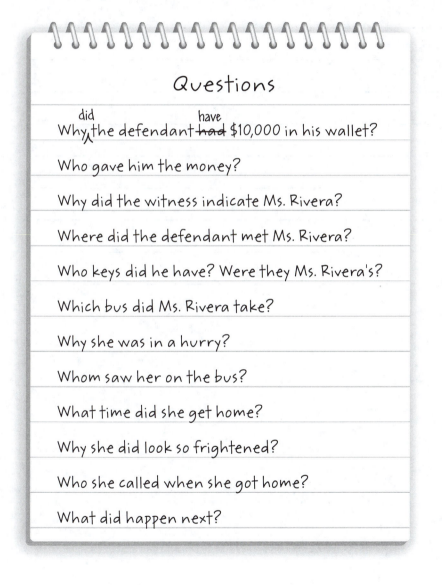

Questions

                did   have
Why the defendant had $10,000 in his wallet?

Who gave him the money?

Why did the witness indicate Ms. Rivera?

Where did the defendant met Ms. Rivera?

Who keys did he have? Were they Ms. Rivera's?

Which bus did Ms. Rivera take?

Why she was in a hurry?

Whom saw her on the bus?

What time did she get home?

Why she did look so frightened?

Who she called when she got home?

What did happen next?

EXERCISE 5 PERSONAL WRITING

Imagine that a friend has just moved. Write your friend an email and ask questions about his or her new home. Use some of the *wh-* question words from the box.

| How far | What | Where | Who |
| How many | When | Which | Why |

EXAMPLE: Hi Jason,

I just found out that you moved. How's your new home? I hope you like it. When did you move in? What does it look like? I know you wanted more space. How many . . .

_____

_____

_____

_____

_____

_____

_____

_____

_____

EXERCISE 1 AFFIRMATIVE AND NEGATIVE STATEMENTS WITH *BE GOING TO*

Look at Mr. and Mrs. Taylor's boarding passes. Then read the sentences. All of them have incorrect information. Correct the information.

1. Mr. Taylor is going to go to Los Angeles.

   He isn't going to go to Los Angeles.

   He's going to go to San Francisco.

2. He's going to take the train.

   _____

   _____

3. He's going to travel alone.

   _____

   _____

(continued on next page)

4. The Taylors are going to leave from Chicago.

_____

_____

5. They're going to fly US Airways.

_____

_____

6. They're going to leave on July 11.

_____

_____

7. They're going to take Flight 149.

_____

_____

8. The plane is going to take off at 7:00 a.m.

_____

_____

9. The Taylors are going to sit apart.

_____

_____

10. Mrs. Taylor is going to sit in Seat 15B.

_____

_____

EXERCISE 2 QUESTIONS WITH *BE GOING TO*

Use the words in parentheses to write questions about Mr. and Mrs. Taylor's trip. Use *be going to*.

1. (What / you / do this summer)

   A: *What are you going to do this summer?*

   B: My wife and I are going to take a trip to San Francisco.

2. (How long / you / stay)

   A: _____

   B: Just for a week.

3. (you / stay at a hotel)

   A: _____

   B: Yes. We're staying at a hotel in North Beach.

4. (What / you / do in San Francisco)

   A: _____

   B: Oh, the usual, I suppose. Sightseeing and shopping.

5. (you / visit Fisherman's Wharf)

   A: _____

   B: Yes. We're going to take one of those city bus tours.

6. (your daughter / go with you)

   A: _____

   B: No, she's going to attend summer school. Our son isn't going either.

7. (What / he / do)

   A: _____

   B: He got a job at an Italian restaurant.

8. (When / you / leave)

   A: _____

   B: June 11.

   A: Have a good trip. San Francisco is an incredible city.

   B: Thanks.

EXERCISE 3 AFFIRMATIVE AND NEGATIVE STATEMENTS, QUESTIONS, AND SHORT ANSWERS WITH *WILL*

Mrs. Taylor is reading an interview about personal robots in the airplane magazine. Complete the interview with the verbs in parentheses and *will* or *won't*.

INTERVIEWER: We all know that robots are already working in factories. But tell us something about

the future. _____*Will*_____ people _____*have*_____ robots at home?
                                        1. (have)

SCIENTIST: They already do! There are, for example, small robots that vacuum the floor. I believe

that before too long, personal robots _____ as common in the home as
                                              2. (become)

personal computers are today.

INTERVIEWER: _____ they _____ the computer?
                                      3. (replace)

SCIENTIST: No, they _____ the computer; but one day, robots _____
                        4. (replace)

probably _____ computers.
              5. (operate)

INTERVIEWER: That's amazing! What other things _____ personal robots

_____?
    6. (do)

SCIENTIST: Well, for one thing, they _____ complete home entertainment centers.
                                            7. (be)

They _____, they _____ . . .
          8. (sing)   **9. (dance)**

INTERVIEWER: _____ they _____ jokes?
                                      10. (tell)

SCIENTIST: Yes, they _____ ! But, as with humans, they _____ always
                        11.

_____ funny!
    12. (be)

INTERVIEWER: What else _____ personal robots _____?
                                                              13. (do)

_____ they _____ more serious uses?
                          14. (have)

SCIENTIST: Yes, they _____ . Robots _____ probably
                        15.

_____ care for this country's aging population. I don't believe they
    16. (help)

_____ people, but they _____ some of the more routine
    17. (replace)   **18. (perform)**

activities such as making the bed and loading the dishwasher.

INTERVIEWER: It all sounds great. Do you predict any problems?

SCIENTIST: Unfortunately, yes. Some people _____ happy with the spread of robots.
                                                  19. (be)

Not everyone's life _____ . Some people _____ their jobs
                          20. (improve)   **21. (lose)**

to robots. And other people _____ criminal robots!
                                  22. (create)

38 Unit 6

INTERVIEWER: _____ we _____ new laws to deal with robotic crime?
23. (need)

SCIENTIST: I'm afraid so.

INTERVIEWER: Tell me, how _____ these personal robots _____ ?
24. (look)

SCIENTIST: Well, they _____ *exactly* like humans, but they _____ us
25. (look)   26. (resemble)

quite a bit.

INTERVIEWER: And when _____ all this _____ ?
27. (happen)

SCIENTIST: Soon! I predict it _____ in the very near future. In fact, I'm sure you
28. (happen)

_____ some of it yourself!
29. (experience)

EXERCISE 4 RECOGNIZING THE SIMPLE PRESENT AND PRESENT PROGRESSIVE WHEN THEY REFER TO THE FUTURE

Read this article about a new play. Underline the simple present and present progressive verbs only when they refer to the future.

CURTAIN CALL

A NEW PLAY

Next Wednesday <u>is</u> the first performance of *Robots* at Town Theater. Melissa Robins is playing the leading role. Robins, who lives in Italy and who is vacationing in Greece, is not available for an interview at this time. She is, however, appearing on Channel 8's *Theater Talk* sometime next month.

Although shows traditionally begin at 8:00 p.m., *Robots*, because of its length, starts half an hour earlier. Immediately following the opening-night performance, the cast is having a reception in the theater lounge. *Robots* was a huge success in London, where all performances quickly sold out, but tickets are still available at Town Theater through March 28th. Call 555–6310 for more information.

EXERCISE 5 CONTRAST OF FUTURE FORMS

Some people are flying to San Francisco. Read the conversations and circle the most appropriate future forms.

1. A: Do you know our arrival time?

    B: According to the itinerary, we arrive / (we'll arrive) at 10:45.

2. A: Why did you bring your computer with you?

    B: I'll do / I'm going to do some work while we're away.

3. A: I'm thirsty. I think I'll ask / I'm asking for a soda.

    B: Good idea. There's the flight attendant.

4. A: Excuse me. Do you know what the weather is like in San Francisco?

    B: It's clear now, but it's raining / it's going to rain tomorrow.

5. A: Oh, good! They'll show / They're showing the new *Star Wars* on today's flight.

    B: Great! I missed it when it was playing in the theaters.

6. A: Just look at those dark clouds!

    B: Yes, it looks like we're going to have / we'll have some rough weather ahead.

7. A: Be careful! Hold on to your cup! It's at the edge of your tray, and it looks like it'll spill / it's going to spill.

    B: I've got it. This sure is a bumpy flight!

    A: I know. I'll be / I'm glad to be back on the ground again.

8. A: I'm tired. I think I'll take / I'm taking a little nap. Wake me when the movie begins.

    B: OK. Sweet dreams.

9. A: It's 11:00 p.m. already!

    B: I know. We're going to arrive / We arrive late.

    A: Really? I'm surprised. We took off on time.

10. A: You know, I don't think the airport buses run after midnight.

    B: I'm afraid you're right. How are we going to get / are we getting to the hotel?

11. **A:** Hmmm. No buses. Well, that's no problem. <u>We'll take</u> / <u>We're going to take</u> a taxi.

   B: Do you think there <u>will still be</u> / <u>are still</u> taxis in front of the terminal so late?

   A: Oh, sure.

12. **A:** I missed the announcement. What did the captain say?

   B: He said, "Fasten your seat belts. <u>We're landing</u> / <u>We'll land</u> in about 10 minutes."

13. **C:** How long <u>are you going to stay</u> / <u>will you stay</u> in San Francisco?

   A: Just a week.

   C: Well, enjoy yourselves, and thank you for flying FairAir.

14. **A:** Maybe <u>we'll see</u> / <u>we're seeing</u> you on the return flight!

   C: Maybe!

EXERCISE 6 CONTRAST OF FUTURE FORMS

Complete the conversation with the correct future form of the verbs in parentheses. There will often be more than one correct answer. Use contractions when possible.

JASON: What _____*are*_____ we _____*doing*_____ tonight, Mom?
                                                    1. (do)

MOM: We _____ a play after dinner. I got tickets before we left. Remember?
                  2. (see)

DAD: What time _____ we _____ to be at the theater?
                                      3. (need)

MOM: The play _____ at 8:00, so I think we _____ there around
                      4. (start)   **5.** (get)

   15 minutes before.

JASON: What about dinner? Where _____ we _____?
                                                        6. (eat)

MOM: We _____ dinner at a restaurant on Fisherman's Wharf. We have reservations
              7. (have)

   for 6:00.

JASON: How _____ we _____ there?
                                8. (get)

MOM: Well, according to this schedule, the hotel van _____ for downtown at 5:00.
                                                            9. (leave)

DAD: Hey, look at those clouds! It looks like it _____.
                                                    10. (rain)

MOM: No problem. We _____ our umbrellas.
                        11. (take)

DAD: You know, I'm tired. I think I _____ down for a while before dinner.
                                        12. (lie)

MOM: Good idea. I _____ you in about a half hour.
                        13. (wake)

JASON: I'm really excited. This _____ a great vacation!
                                      14. (be)

EXERCISE 7 EDITING

Read Jason's postcard. There are five mistakes in the use of future forms. The first mistake is already corrected. Find and correct four more. There may be more than one way to correct the mistakes.

Greetings from San Francisco

Hi!

~~I going~~ I'm going to stay here for a week with my parents. Our hotel is incredible, and I spent the afternoon floating in the pool.

We have a lot of fun things planned. Tonight we'll see a play called *Robots*. Mom already bought the tickets for it. The play begins at 7:30, and before that we have dinner on Fisherman's Wharf. Right now we're still in the hotel, but we'll have to leave soon. It's good that we're going to be indoors most of the time because the sky is getting very dark. It will rain!

I call you soon.

Jason

EXERCISE 8 PERSONAL WRITING

Imagine you are on vacation. Write a postcard to a friend. Tell your friend about your plans. Use some of the words and phrases from the box.

for our next vacation	soon
in a few minutes	tomorrow
next week	tonight

EXAMPLE: Hi Rosa,

I'm on vacation in Florida with my family. The weather is great, and we have a lot of nice things planned. Tonight we're going to . . .

_____

_____

_____

_____

_____

_____

_____

_____

_____

_____

_____

Future Time Clauses

EXERCISE 1 SIMPLE PRESENT OR FUTURE WITH *WILL*

Complete the clauses with the correct form of the verbs in parentheses. Use the future or the simple present. Then match the time clauses to the main clauses.

Time Clause

_h_ 1. When the alarm clock _____rings_____ at 7:00 a.m.,
(ring)

_____ 2. After she _____,
(get up)

_____ 3. As soon as the coffee _____
(be)
ready,

_____ 4. While they _____ breakfast,
(eat)

_____ 5. When they _____ breakfast,
(finish)

_____ 6. After her husband _____
(wash)
the dishes,

_____ 7. As soon as they _____ the
(get in)
car,

_____ 8. Until he _____ his driver's
(get)
license,

_____ 9. Until the rain _____,
(stop)

_____ 10. By the time the day _____
(be)
over,

Main Clause

a. they _____
(be)
very tired.

b. she _____.
(drive)

c. they _____ it.
(drink)

d. they _____ their
(fasten)
seat belts.

e. she _____ them.
(dry)

f. they _____ their
(need)
umbrellas.

g. they _____ the
(do)
dishes.

h̶. she _____'ll get up_____.
(get up)

i. she _____
(take)
a shower.

j. they _____ the
(read)
morning newspaper.

EXERCISE 2 SIMPLE PRESENT OR FUTURE (*WILL / BE GOING TO*) AND TIME EXPRESSIONS

Vera is a student. Look at her future plans. (The events are in order.) Complete the sentences below with the correct form of the verbs in parentheses. Use Vera's plans to choose the correct time expression.

Future Plans
Take the TOEFL[1] exam
Apply to college for next year
Finish high school
Visit Aunt Isabel
Get a summer job and take a computer programming course
Fly to Brazil —— Aug. 28
Attend Sonia's wedding —— Sept. 5
Return to the United States
Move into new apartment
Look for a part-time job

[1] *TOEFL*®: Test of English as a Foreign Language

1. Vera ___will take___ the TOEFL exam ___before___ she ___applies___
   (take)   (when / before)   (apply)
   to college.

2. Vera _____ to college _____ she _____ school.
        (apply)   (before / after)   (finish)

3. _____ she _____ school, she _____ her aunt.
   (before / after)   (finish)   (visit)

4. _____ she _____ at a summer job, she _____
   (before / while)   (work)   (take)
   a course in computer programming.

5. She _____ her aunt Isabel _____ she _____ a job.
       (visit)   (while / before)   (get)

6. _____ she _____ the course, she _____ to Brazil.
   (before / when)   (finish)   (fly)

7. She _____ Sonia's wedding _____ she _____ in
       (attend)   (when / before)   (be)
   Brazil next September.

(continued on next page)

8. She _____ to the United States _____ she _____
     (return)   (before / after)   (attend)

Sonia's wedding.

9. She _____ into a new apartment _____ she _____ to
     (move)   (when / while)   (return)

the United States.

10. _____ she _____ into her new apartment, Vera
     (before / after)   (move)

_____ a part-time job.
     (look for)

EXERCISE 3 SENTENCE COMBINING

Combine these pairs of sentences. Use *will* or *be going to* and the simple present for the
future. Remember to use commas when necessary.

1. Vera will finish her summer job. Then she's going to fly to Brazil.

     Vera is going to fly to Brazil _____ after *she finishes her summer job.* _____

2. Vera will save enough money from her job. Then she's going to buy a plane ticket.

     As soon as _____

3. Vera's going to buy presents for her family. Then she's going to go home.

     Before _____

4. Vera will arrive at the airport. Her father will be there to drive her home.

     When _____

5. Vera and her father will get home. They'll immediately have dinner.

     As soon as _____

6. They'll finish dinner. Then Vera will give her family the presents.

     _____ after _____

7. Vera's brother will wash the dishes. Vera's sister will dry them.

     _____ while _____

8. The whole family is going to stay up talking. Then the clock will strike midnight.

     _____ until _____

9. They'll all feel very tired. Then they'll go to bed.

     By the time _____

10. Vera's head will hit the pillow. She'll fall asleep immediately.

_____ as soon as _____

11. Vera will wake up the next morning. She's going to call her friends.

When _____

12. She'll have breakfast. Then she'll see her friends.

_____ as soon as _____

EXERCISE 4 EDITING

Read Vera's journal entry. There are seven mistakes in the use of future time clauses.
The first one is already corrected. Find and correct six more. Remember to look at
punctuation!

> I have a lot of goals, but I need to get more organized if I
> want to achieve them. So, tomorrow I'm going to start working
> on them. College is my number one goal. As soon as I ~~will~~ get up,
> I'm going to download some online college catalogs. After I
> examine them carefully, I choose a few schools that interest me
> and I try to set up some visits. Maybe I can even get some
> interviews with some teachers at the school. When I'm going to
> visit the schools, I'll also try to speak to other students. That's
> always a good way to find out about a place. After I'm seeing
> several schools, I decide which ones to apply to. When I get
> accepted, I'll make the best choice. While I'm in school, I'll study
> hard and in four years I have my degree!

EXERCISE 5 PERSONAL WRITING

Write a paragraph about your goals. Use some of the phrases from the box.

After I . . ., I . . .	I won't . . . before I . . .
As soon as I . . ., I . . .	When I . . ., I . . .
Before I do that, I . . .	While I . . ., I . . .

EXAMPLE: One of my goals is to save enough money to buy a used car. When I finish school, I'm going to look for a job. While I'm working, I'll . . .

_____

_____

_____

_____

_____

_____

_____

_____

_____

_____

UNIT

8

Present Perfect: *Since* and *For*

EXERCISE 1 SPELLING: REGULAR AND IRREGULAR PAST PARTICIPLES

Write the past participles.

Base Form	Simple Past	Past Participle
1. be	was / were	_____been_____
2. break	broke	_____
3. come	came	_____
4. fall	fell	_____
5. go	went	_____
6. have	had	_____
7. lose	lost	_____
8. play	played	_____
9. watch	watched	_____
10. win	won	_____

EXERCISE 2 *SINCE* OR *FOR*

Complete these sentences with *since* or *for*.

1. I haven't known Ana _____*for*_____ a long time.

2. She has been on my soccer team only _____ last September.

3. We've become good friends _____ then.

4. Our team hasn't been in a game _____ a few weeks.

5. _____ our last game, we've practiced a lot.

6. _____ weeks we've gone to the field every day after class.

7. We haven't lost a game _____ several months.

8. I have loved sports _____ I was a little girl.

EXERCISE 3 AFFIRMATIVE STATEMENTS WITH *SINCE* AND *FOR*

Complete the information about two athletes who have been famous since they were
children. Use the present perfect form of the verbs in parentheses and choose between
since and *for*.

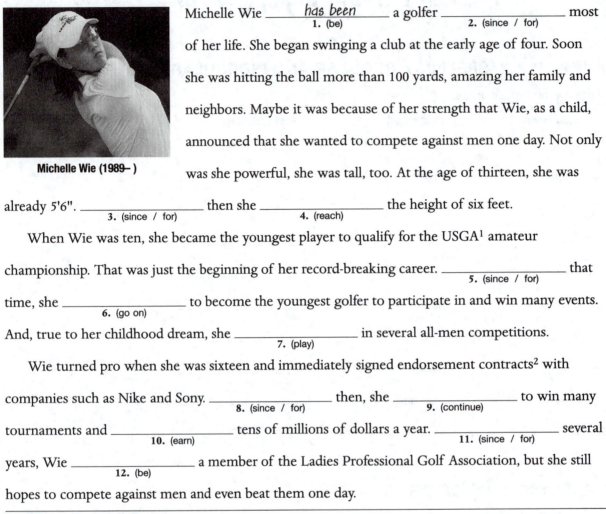

Michelle Wie (1989–)

Michelle Wie ___*has been*___ a golfer _____ most
                 1. (be)   **2. (since / for)**

of her life. She began swinging a club at the early age of four. Soon

she was hitting the ball more than 100 yards, amazing her family and

neighbors. Maybe it was because of her strength that Wie, as a child,

announced that she wanted to compete against men one day. Not only

was she powerful, she was tall, too. At the age of thirteen, she was

already 5'6". _____ then she _____ the height of six feet.
            3. (since / for)   **4. (reach)**

When Wie was ten, she became the youngest player to qualify for the USGA[1] amateur

championship. That was just the beginning of her record-breaking career. _____ that
                                                                        5. (since / for)

time, she _____ to become the youngest golfer to participate in and win many events.
        6. (go on)

And, true to her childhood dream, she _____ in several all-men competitions.
                                      7. (play)

Wie turned pro when she was sixteen and immediately signed endorsement contracts[2] with

companies such as Nike and Sony. _____ then, she _____ to win many
                                8. (since / for)   **9. (continue)**

tournaments and _____ tens of millions of dollars a year. _____ several
              10. (earn)   **11. (since / for)**

years, Wie _____ a member of the Ladies Professional Golf Association, but she still
         12. (be)

hopes to compete against men and even beat them one day.

[1] *USGA:* United States Golf Association
[2] *endorsement contracts:* agreements to do advertisements and TV commercials for a company

Juan Martín del Potro (1988–)

Born in Tandil, Argentina, Juan Martín del Potro, known as "Delpo,"

_____ a tennis player _____ he was seven. He
13. (be)   **14. (since / for)**

won his first senior match at the young age of fifteen, and he

_____ to win many competitions _____ that
15. (continue)   **16. (since / for)**

time.

Del Potro turned pro in 2005. _____ 2006, he
                            17. (since / for)

_____ many records—frequently finishing the year as the
18. (break)

youngest player in the top 100. In 2008, he won four titles in a row, and in

2009, he finished in the top ten. He _____ also _____ millions of dollars
                                                                    19. (win)

in prize money _____ he turned pro.
                  20. (since / for)

    The road to success has not been always easy. _____ many years, del Potro
                                                                      21. (since / for)

_____ a lot of physical problems and he _____ playing many times
     22. (have)   23. (stop)

because of injuries. But he always comes back. His long-time dream was to win the U.S. Open. In

2009, his dream came true. Not only did he win, but he beat Roger Federer, the number one tennis

player in the world at the time.

    "_____ I was young," said the twenty-year-old 6'6" star, "I _____ of
         24. (since / for)   25. (dream)

winning this trophy . . . It's an unbelievable moment . . . Everything is perfect." Unfortunately,

_____ 2010, del Potro _____ as much because of a wrist injury.
   26. (since / for)   27. (not compete)

EXERCISE 4 QUESTIONS AND ANSWERS

Use the words in parentheses to write questions about the athletes in Exercise 3. Look at
the information again and answer the questions.

1. (How long / Michelle Wie / be a golfer)

   A: _How long has Michelle Wie been a golfer?_____

   B: _She has been a golfer since she was four years old_ OR _for most of her life._____

2. (How long / she / have a record-breaking career)

   A: _____

   B: _____

3. (How long / she / be a professional golfer)

   A: _____

   B: _____

4. (she / have any endorsement contracts)

   A: _____

   B: _____

5. (How long / Juan Martín del Potro / be a tennis player)

   A: _____

   B: _____

(continued on next page)

6. (How much money / he / win since he turned pro)

A: _____

B: _____

7. (What kind of problems / he / have for years)

A: _____

B: _____

8. (he / win any titles since 2008)

A: _____

B: _____

EXERCISE 5 AFFIRMATIVE AND NEGATIVE STATEMENTS

Read each pair of sentences. Use the correct present perfect form to write or complete a summary sentence that has a similar meaning.

1. A: Jack and Victor became golfers in 2009.

B: They are still golfers.

SUMMARY: _Jack and Victor have been golfers_ _____ since 2009.

2. A: Fei-Mei and Natasha competed in 2010.

B: That was the last time they competed.

SUMMARY: _Fei-Mei and Natasha haven't competed since 2010._ _____

3. A: Min Ho won two awards in 2014.

B: He won one other award in 2015.

SUMMARY: _____ since 2014.

4. A: Marilyn entered a competition in 2014.

B: She entered one more competition last year.

SUMMARY: _____ since 2014.

5. A: Victor and Marilyn saw each other in 2015.

B: That was the last time they saw each other.

SUMMARY: _____

6. A: Karl became a tennis player in 2014.

   B: He is still a tennis player.

   SUMMARY: _____

7. A: Karl lost two tournaments in February of this year.

   B: He lost another tournament last week.

   SUMMARY: _____ since February of this year.

8. A: Andreas went to a tennis match two years ago.

   B: That was the last match he went to.

   SUMMARY: _____ for two years.

EXERCISE 6 EDITING

Read these online tweets[1] about sports. There are eight mistakes in the use of the present perfect with *since* and *for*. The first is already corrected. Find and correct seven more.

    • • •

What a great game! Marissa has been my favorite ~~since~~ *for* years!

I heard that Taylor got $350,000 for winning yesterday's tournament. How much money does he make since he turned pro? Does anyone know?

Do you think Lee can support himself playing golf? He hasn't win a major tournament for two years. That's a long time!

Karla didn't win a game since last year. I really feel bad for her.

Walter has stopped playing twice since January because of injuries. That's really too bad.

I haven't had the opportunity to attend a competition since three years. This one is awesome!

I used to think golf was boring. Not anymore. I don't enjoy a sports event so much for years!

I think Pedro's game has improve dramatically since he won the last tournament.

Antonio's positive attitude have helped him improve his game since he lost the match last month. I consider him a role model.

---

[1] **tweets:** very short messages on the social media website Twitter™

EXERCISE 7 PERSONAL WRITING

Write about someone you know who plays sports. (You can also write about yourself.) Use some of the phrases from the box.

for a long time	since he / she / I
for . . . years	since then . . .
since 20__	since . . . not . . .

EXAMPLE: My friend Karl has been on the school basketball team for two years. His team has won many games since . . .

_____

_____

_____

_____

_____

_____

_____

_____

_____

_____

Present Perfect: *Already, Yet,* and *Still*

EXERCISE 1 SPELLING: REGULAR AND IRREGULAR PAST PARTICIPLES

Write the past participles.

Base Form	Simple Past	Past Participle
1. act	acted	*acted*
2. become	became	
3. choose	chose	
4. clean	cleaned	
5. dance	danced	
6. drink	drank	
7. fight	fought	
8. find	found	
9. get	got	
10. give	gave	
11. hold	held	
12. keep	kept	
13. know	knew	
14. look	looked	
15. plan	planned	
16. sing	sang	
17. smile	smiled	
18. throw	threw	

EXERCISE 2 QUESTIONS AND STATEMENTS WITH *ALREADY, YET, AND STILL*

Complete the conversation with the correct form of the verbs in parentheses and an adverb—*already, yet,* or *still*. Use contractions if possible.

TED: I hear you're looking for a new apartment. ___Have___ you ___found___ one
                         1.   **2.** (find)

   ___yet___?
   3. (already / yet / still)

MIA: No, and we're getting discouraged. We _____ _____
                                          4.   **5.** (already / yet / still)

   _____ at more than 10, and we _____ _____ one
   6. (look)   **7.** (already / yet / still)   **8.** (not find)

   that we like!

TED: Well, don't give up. I _____ _____ _____ at least 20.
                                9.   **10.** (already / yet / still)   **11.** (see)

   Are you working with a real estate agent? It may be time to get some professional help.

MIA: No. We wanted to try to find something ourselves, so we _____ to an agent
                                                        12. (not go)

   _____. But I think you're right. We may be more successful with an agent.
   13. (already / yet / still)

   Unfortunately, we _____ _____ _____ a lot of time
                             14.   **15.** (already / yet / still)   **16.** (waste)

   looking at apartments that were completely wrong for us.

TED: I know what you mean. _____ you _____ on a specific
                              17.   **18.** (decide)

   neighborhood _____?
   19. (already / yet / still)

MIA: No. We _____ our minds _____. What about you? Where do you
         20. (not make up)   **21.** (already / yet / still)

   want to move?

TED: Actually, we'd really like to stay in this neighborhood. We just need a bigger place.

MIA: Well, good luck!

TED: Thanks. You, too.

EXERCISE 3 QUESTIONS AND ANSWERS WITH *ALREADY, YET,* AND *STILL*

Mia is going to move. She is very organized. Read her list of things to do. She has checked (✓) all the things she's already done. Write questions and answers about the words in parentheses.

Moving Checklist

- ☑ choose a moving company
- ☐ find a professional painter
- ☑ collect boxes for packing
- ☑ get a change-of-address form from the post office
- ☐ begin to pack clothes
- ☑ make a list of cleaning supplies
- ☐ clean the refrigerator and stove
- ☑ buy two bookcases
- ☑ give away the old couch
- ☐ buy a new couch
- ☐ throw away old magazines
- ☐ invite the neighbors over for a good-bye party

1. A: (moving company) *Has she chosen a moving company yet?*

   B: *Yes, she's already chosen a moving company.*

2. A: (clothes) *Has she begun to pack clothes yet?*

   B: *No, she hasn't begun to pack clothes yet.* OR *She still hasn't begun to pack clothes.*

3. A: (bookcases) _____

   B: _____

4. A: (magazines) _____

   B: _____

5. A: (painter) _____

   B: _____

(continued on next page)

6. A: (boxes) _____

   B: _____

7. A: (new couch) _____

   B: _____

8. A: (old couch) _____

   B: _____

9. A: (refrigerator and stove) _____

   B: _____

10. A: (cleaning supplies) _____

   B: _____

11. A: (change-of-address form) _____

   B: _____

12. A: (the neighbors) _____

   B: _____

EXERCISE 4 EDITING

Mia sent an email to her friend. There are seven mistakes in the use of the present perfect with *already, yet,* and *still*. The first one is already corrected. Find and correct six more.

● ● ●

Hi!

I'm writing to you from our new apartment! It took us a long time to find, but finally, with

some professional advice, we were successful. We've already ~~be~~ _been_ here two weeks, and

we feel very much at home. But there's still a lot to do. Believe it or not, we haven't

unpacked all the boxes still! We took most of our old furniture, so we don't need to get

too much new stuff. We had to buy a new couch for the living room, but they haven't

delivered it already.

We've already meet some of our new neighbors. They seem very nice. One of them have

already invited us over for coffee.

Had you made vacation plans yet? As soon as we get the couch (it's a sleeper), we'd

love for you to visit. Already we've planned places to take you when you come, but let

us know if there are any specific things you'd like to do or see.

—Mia

EXERCISE 5 PERSONAL WRITING

A. Make a "To Do" list of things you need to do in the next few days or weeks. Include some things you have already done, and check (✓) those things.

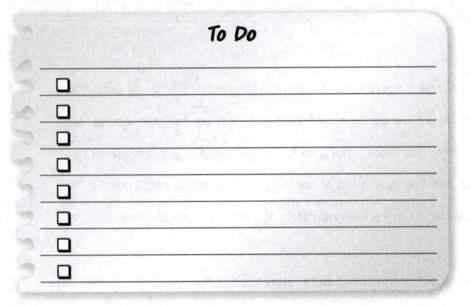

To Do

☐ _____
☐ _____
☐ _____
☐ _____
☐ _____
☐ _____
☐ _____
☐ _____

B. Write an email to a friend. Tell him or her about what you *have already done,* what you *haven't done yet,* and what you *still haven't done.*

EXAMPLE: My cousins are coming to visit this weekend, and I have a lot of things to do before they get here. I've already cleaned the apartment, but I haven't gone shopping for food yet. And I know they'll want to see a play, but I still haven't gotten tickets . . .

_____

_____

_____

_____

_____

_____

_____

_____

_____

_____

EXERCISE 1 SPELLING: REGULAR AND IRREGULAR PAST PARTICIPLES

Write the past participles.

Base Form	Simple Past	Past Participle
1. begin	began	*begun*
2. decide	decided	_____
3. fly	flew	_____
4. go	went	_____
5. hear	heard	_____
6. keep	kept	_____
7. make	made	_____
8. ride	rode	_____
9. see	saw	_____
10. swim	swam	_____
11. travel	traveled	_____
12. work	worked	_____

EXERCISE 2 AFFIRMATIVE STATEMENTS

Complete these statements. Use the present perfect form of the correct verbs from Exercise 1.

1. Julie _____ *has made* _____ several trips this year.

2. You _____ on a camel. Did you enjoy it?

3. I'd like to go to Costa Rica. I _____ that it's beautiful.

4. They _____ the ancient Egyptian pyramids before.

5. He _____ Air France many times. It's his favorite airline.

6. I _____ with dolphins in the ocean. What an adventure!

7. My cousin _____ to go hiking in northern Spain next fall.

8. She _____ hard this year and really needs a vacation.

EXERCISE 3 AFFIRMATIVE AND NEGATIVE STATEMENTS

Read this article about a famous series of travel guides. Complete the sentences with the present perfect form of the verbs in parentheses.

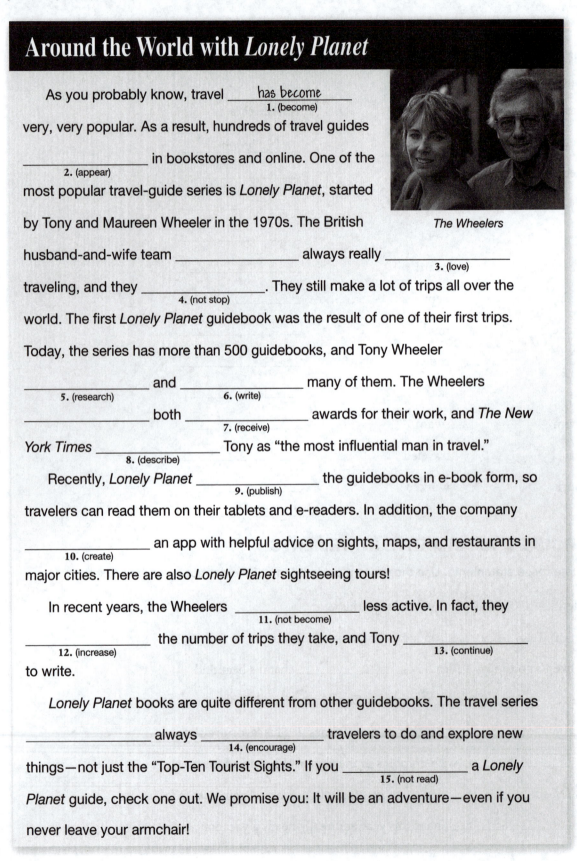

Around the World with *Lonely Planet*

As you probably know, travel _____has become_____

1. (become)

very, very popular. As a result, hundreds of travel guides

_____ in bookstores and online. One of the

2. (appear)

most popular travel-guide series is *Lonely Planet*, started

by Tony and Maureen Wheeler in the 1970s. The British

The Wheelers

husband-and-wife team _____ always really _____

3. (love)

traveling, and they _____. They still make a lot of trips all over the

4. (not stop)

world. The first *Lonely Planet* guidebook was the result of one of their first trips.

Today, the series has more than 500 guidebooks, and Tony Wheeler

_____ and _____ many of them. The Wheelers

5. (research)   **6.** (write)

_____ both _____ awards for their work, and *The New*

7. (receive)

York Times _____ Tony as "the most influential man in travel."

8. (describe)

Recently, *Lonely Planet* _____ the guidebooks in e-book form, so

9. (publish)

travelers can read them on their tablets and e-readers. In addition, the company

_____ an app with helpful advice on sights, maps, and restaurants in

10. (create)

major cities. There are also *Lonely Planet* sightseeing tours!

In recent years, the Wheelers _____ less active. In fact, they

11. (not become)

_____ the number of trips they take, and Tony _____

12. (increase)   **13.** (continue)

to write.

Lonely Planet books are quite different from other guidebooks. The travel series

_____ always _____ travelers to do and explore new

14. (encourage)

things—not just the "Top-Ten Tourist Sights." If you _____ a *Lonely*

15. (not read)

Planet guide, check one out. We promise you: It will be an adventure—even if you

never leave your armchair!

EXERCISE 4 QUESTIONS AND ANSWERS WITH ADVERBS AND TIME EXPRESSIONS

A travel agent is talking to a client. Complete the travel agent's questions with the words in parentheses. Use the agent's notes and the correct adverb or time expression from the box to answer the questions. You will use some words more than once.

many times	never	not lately	once	recently	twice

Adventure Travel Inc.

Egypt—2x
Europe—more than 10x
African safari—(returned two
months ago)
Costa Rica—1x (2004)
China—no

hot-air ballooning—no
dolphin swim—6x or more

group tour—no (and <u>not</u> interested)

1. **AGENT:** <u>Have you ever been</u> _____ to Egypt?
   (ever / be)

   CLIENT: <u>I've been to Egypt twice.</u> _____

2. **AGENT:** _____ Europe?
   (How many times / visit)

   CLIENT: _____

3. **AGENT:** _____ on an African safari?
   (ever / be)

   CLIENT: _____

4. **AGENT:** _____ to Costa Rica?
   (ever / be)

   CLIENT: _____

5. **AGENT:** _____ there?
   (How often / be)

   CLIENT: _____

(continued on next page)

6. AGENT: _____ in China?
(ever / travel)

CLIENT: _____

7. AGENT: _____ in a hot-air balloon?
(ever / go up)

CLIENT: _____

8. AGENT: _____ with dolphins?
(ever / swim)

CLIENT: _____

9. AGENT: _____ a group tour?
(ever / take)

CLIENT: _____.

And I never want to!

EXERCISE 5 EDITING

Read these questions and answers posted on a travel website. There are nine mistakes in the use of the present perfect and adverbs. The first one is already corrected. Find and correct eight more.

TRAVEL WITH CAL

                                         ever been
Q: Have you ~~been ever~~ to Barcelona? I'm planning a trip there this summer and would love some tips.

A: I've never been there, but you can find a lot of useful information on websites such as tripadvisor.com.

Q: I've returned last week from a safari in Africa. It was awesome, and I'm really interested in sharing photos with other travelers. Any ideas?

A: Yes! We've recently formed an online discussion group on safaris and we post photos there. Contact me at travcal@oal.com for more information.

Q: I'm trying to choose a hotel for my trip to Toronto. Has anyone you know ever stays at the Victoria?

A: I've several times stayed there myself. It's convenient and affordable. I think you'd like it.

Q: I'm going to be traveling alone in the south of France. What's the best form of transportation for getting around? I can't afford to rent a car.

A: I've always took local buses. They're comfortable and you get to see a lot of the countryside.

Q: Have you read the results of *Travel Today*'s annual survey? It seems like a lot of people has decided to take vacations closer to home. And many people have choose not to go away at all this summer.

A: Not me! I've booked just a vacation to Australia. I've never was to that part of the world, and I can't wait to go!

EXERCISE 6 PERSONAL WRITING

Write a paragraph about your own travel experiences. Use the present perfect with some of the words from the box.

always	just	many times	never	not . . . lately	often	recently	twice

EXAMPLE: There are so many places I would like to visit. I've never been to Asia, and I've always wanted to see . . .

_____

_____

_____

_____

_____

_____

_____

_____

_____

_____

Present Perfect and Simple Past

EXERCISE 1 SPELLING: REGULAR AND IRREGULAR VERBS

Write the correct form of the verbs.

Base Form	Simple Past	Past Participle
1. be	was / were	*been*
2. _____	became	become
3. begin	began	_____
4. _____	bought	bought
5. decide	_____	_____
6. feel	_____	felt
7. _____	_____	gotten
8. give	_____	_____
9. go	_____	_____
10. have	_____	had
11. _____	lived	_____
12. _____	made	made
13. meet	_____	_____
14. move	_____	_____
15. pay	_____	_____
16. read	_____	_____
17. rise	rose	_____
18. _____	_____	seen
19. start	_____	_____
20. _____	_____	taken

EXERCISE 2 PRESENT PERFECT OR SIMPLE PAST

Complete the sentences about Tom Dorsey, a teacher who is looking for a job in another city.

Last Year	This Year
1. Tom answered 20 employment ads.	_Tom has answered_ 30 ads.
2. _Tom had_ two job interviews.	Tom has had three job interviews.
3. Tom went on one out-of-town interview.	_____ on three out-of-town interviews.
4. _____ one job offer.	Tom has gotten three job offers.
5. Tom made $45,000.	_____ the same amount of money.
6. _____ a lot of interesting people.	Tom has met a lot of interesting people, too.
7. Tom was sick once.	_____ sick twice.
8. _____ well.	Tom has looked tired.
9. _____ a new smartphone.	Tom has bought a smart TV.
10. Tom paid with cash.	_____ by credit card.
11. Tom read five books.	_____ two books.
12. Tom didn't manage to take a vacation.	_____ to take two short vacations. He's been to Florida and southern California.
13. Tom didn't give any parties.	_____ two parties.
14. _____ a little discouraged.	Tom has felt a lot more encouraged.

EXERCISE 3 PRESENT PERFECT OR SIMPLE PAST

A journalist is interviewing a woman about marriage. Complete the interview with the correct form of the verbs in parentheses. Use the present perfect or the simple past.

JOURNALIST: How long _____*have*_____ you _____*been*_____ married?
1. (be)

WOMAN: Tom and I _____ married in 2014, so we _____ married for
2. (get)   3. (be)

just a few years.

JOURNALIST: And when _____ you _____ your first child?
4. (have)

WOMAN: Well, I _____ a mother pretty quickly. We _____ Stephanie
5. (become)   6. (have)

10 months after we _____ married.
7. (be)

JOURNALIST: You say this isn't your first marriage. How long _____ your first marriage

_____?
8. (last)

WOMAN: About two years. We _____ in 2012.
9. (divorce)

JOURNALIST: _____ the two of you _____ any kids?
10. (have)

WOMAN: No, we _____.
11.

JOURNALIST: Do you still see your first husband?

WOMAN: Yes. We _____ to stay friends. In fact, I _____ him last
12. (manage)   13. (see)

week. He and Tom _____ friends, too. It's a nice arrangement.
14. (become)

JOURNALIST: _____ he _____?
15. (remarry)

WOMAN: No, he _____. But I'm sure it's just a temporary situation.
16.

JOURNALIST: In your opinion, why _____ your first marriage _____?
17. (fail)

WOMAN: I think that we _____ married too young. We _____ each
18. (get)   19. (not know)

other well enough.

JOURNALIST: Where _____ you _____ Tom?
20. (meet)

WOMAN: In Atlanta. We _____ both students there.
21. (be)

JOURNALIST: And when _____ you _____ to Los Angeles?
22. (move)

WOMAN: Last year. Los Angeles is the third city we _____ in! Tom is a college
23. (live)

professor, and it's hard to find a permanent job these days. So, when he gets a job offer,

he really can't turn it down. We don't like moving so often, so I hope this is just a

temporary solution to the job problem.

EXERCISE 4 PRESENT PERFECT OR SIMPLE PAST

Read some facts about the changing American family. Complete the sentences with the present perfect or simple past form of the verbs from the boxes.

begin	~~change~~	get	have

The American family ___*has changed*___ a lot since the 1960s. In the 1960s, couples
1.

_____ to get married at an older age. They also _____ divorced more
2. 3.

frequently than they ever did, and they _____ fewer children.
4.

be	create	occur	rise

Age

In 1960, the average age for a first marriage for women _____ 20.3 and for men 22.8.
5.

Today, it _____ to 26 for women and 28 for men. In the early 1960s, most divorces
6.

_____ among couples older than 45. Today, people of all ages are getting divorced at a
7.

very high rate. This, in part, _____ many single-parent homes.
8.

be	have	increase	start

Birth Rate

In the mid-1960s, birth rates _____ to drop. Then, almost 6 percent of women
9.

_____ three or more children by the time they _____ in their late 30s.
10. 11.

These days, 35 percent of women in the same age group have only two children. In addition, the

number of births to older women _____ greatly _____.
12.

change	get	reach	stay

Living Arrangements

Before 1960, most children _____ in their parents' homes until they
13.

_____ married. This pattern _____ since then. Today, many single
14. 15.

people live alone. Also affecting today's living arrangements is the fact that life expectancy

_____ an all-time high of 79 years. This means that there are a lot more older people,
16.

and some of them are moving in with their adult children.

EXERCISE 5 EDITING

Read Diana's email to a friend. There are eight mistakes in the use of the present perfect and the simple past. The first mistake is already corrected. Find and correct seven more.

Hi Jennifer—

met
Last month, I ~~have met~~ the most wonderful guy. His name is Roger, and he's a student in my night

class. He lived here since 2014. Before that, he lived in Detroit, too—so we have a lot in common.

Roger has been married for five years but got divorced last April.

Roger and I managed to spend a lot of time together in spite of our busy schedules. Last week, I

saw him every night, and this week we already gotten together three times after class. I find that I

miss him when we're apart!

Monday night we have seen a great movie. Did you see *The Purple Room*? It's playing in all the

theaters now.

We've decided to take a trip back to Detroit in the summer. Maybe we can get together. It would

be great to see you again. Please let me know if you'll be there.

Love,

Diana

P.S. Here's a photo of Roger that I've taken a few weeks ago.

EXERCISE 6 PERSONAL WRITING

Write one or two paragraphs about how your life has changed in the past few years. Use some of the phrases from the box with the present perfect or simple past.

Five years ago, . . .	Lately . . .
For the past two years, . . .	Last year . . .
Since 20__	This year . . .

EXAMPLE: My life has really changed a lot in the past few years. Five years ago, I only had a few friends here, but since I . . .

_____

_____

_____

_____

_____

_____

_____

_____

_____

_____

_____

_____

_____

UNIT 12

Present Perfect Progressive and Present Perfect

EXERCISE 1 PRESENT PERFECT PROGRESSIVE STATEMENTS

Read the information about Amanda and Pete Kelly. Write a sentence—affirmative or negative—that summarizes the information. Use the present perfect progressive with *since* or *for.*

1. It's 9:00. Amanda began working at 7:00. She is still working.

   Amanda has been working since 7:00 OR *for two hours.*

2. She is writing articles about global warming. She began a series last month.

   _____

3. Amanda and Pete used to live in New York. They left New York a few years ago.

   _____

4. They are now living in Toronto. They moved there in 2013.

   _____

5. They drive a fuel-efficient car. They got it last year.

   _____

6. Pete lost his job last year. He isn't working now.

   _____

7. Pete and Amanda are thinking of traveling to Africa. They began thinking about this last year.

   _____

8. Amanda is reading a lot about Africa. She started a few months ago.

   _____

9. Pete went back to school last month. He's studying zoology.[1]

   _____

10. Amanda and Pete started looking for a new apartment a month ago. They're still looking.

    _____

---

[1] *zoology:* the scientific study of animals and their behavior

EXERCISE 2 PRESENT PERFECT PROGRESSIVE OR PRESENT PERFECT

Read the article about a famous Canadian scientist and environmentalist. Complete the information with the present perfect progressive or present perfect form of the verbs in parentheses. If both forms are possible, use the present perfect progressive.

Making a World of Difference

Born in 1936 in Vancouver, Canada, David Suzuki is a well-known scientist and a radio and TV broadcaster.[1] He __has__ also __become__ one of the
1. (become)
most famous environmentalists in the world. Dr. Suzuki

_____ more than 40 books about
2. (write)
nature and the environment, including books on these topics for children. In acknowledgement of his accomplishments, he _____ many awards, among them the United
3. (win)
Nations Environmental Program medal. Suzuki holds several academic degrees and is an expert in the fields of genetics (the study of how the qualities of living things are passed on through the genes) and zoology (the study of animals and their behavior). He taught for many years before retiring in 2001. Since his retirement, he

_____ a professor emeritus[2] at the University of British Columbia.
4. (be)
In addition, he _____ more than 20 honorary degrees[3] for his work.
5. (receive)

In 1990, he started the David Suzuki Foundation. One of the organization's goals is to educate people about environmental issues and encourage them to change behaviors that are harmful to the Earth. For over two decades, the David Suzuki Foundation

_____ to protect Canada's climate and to reverse global warming.
6. (work)
It also _____ young people about the importance of a healthy
7. (teach)
environment.

---

[1] **broadcaster:** someone who speaks on radio and television programs
[2] **professor emeritus:** a professor who is no longer working but still has an official title
[3] **honorary degrees:** degrees a college or university gives to someone famous who did not take the courses necessary to receive the degree at the school

On the Foundation's website there are suggestions of everyday actions that people can take to help the environment. Suzuki himself _____ steps to
8. (take)
help save the planet. Lately, in order to use less fuel, he _____
9. (stop)
going on vacations that require air travel. He _____ also

_____ his speaking engagements so that they are geographically
10. (organize)
close, again saving fuel in getting from one place to another.

Above all, Suzuki is probably most famous for his work in television. In his long

career, he _____ and _____ many shows that
11. (design)   **12. (develop)**
teach audiences about the wonders of our world. And since 1960, people in more than

40 countries around the world _____ his very popular TV series
13. (watch)
The Nature of Things.

Now in his eighties, Suzuki

_____ classes
14. (not teach)
at the university, but he

_____
15. (not stop)
educating people about nature and

the results of climate change. He

strongly believes that global

warming is a very serious problem, caused by human activities, and that people must

change their behaviors to save the planet. To spread his message, he

_____ and _____ speeches. By focusing
16. (travel)   **17. (give)**
people's attention on environmental issues through his teaching, writings, speeches,

and shows, David Suzuki _____ a long way in fulfilling his
18. (go)
foundation's mission: "to protect the diversity of nature and our quality of life, now

and for the future."

EXERCISE 3 PRESENT PERFECT PROGRESSIVE OR PRESENT PERFECT

David Suzuki's Foundation has suggestions of things people can do to help the environment. Read the list. Amanda and Pete have checked (✓) the things they do. Write sentences about what they *have been doing* or *haven't been doing* and what they *have done* or *haven't done*. Use the present perfect progressive or present perfect.

Ten Little Things for Big Change

☐ 1. Buy locally grown and produced food.

☑ 2. Eat meat-free meals one day a week.

☐ 3. Don't use pesticides.[1]

☑ 4. Choose energy-efficient appliances.

☑ 5. Reduce home heating and electricity use.

☐ 6. Recycle paper, cans, and bottles.

☑ 7. Buy a fuel-efficient car.

☐ 8. Walk, bike, car pool, or take public transportation.

☐ 9. Choose a home close to work or school.

☐ 10. Take a vacation close to home.

---

[1] *pesticides:* chemicals that kill insects

---

1. *They haven't been buying locally grown and produced food.*

2. _____

3. _____

4. _____

5. _____

6. _____

7. _____

8. _____

9. _____

10. _____

EXERCISE 4 QUESTIONS AND ANSWERS: PRESENT PERFECT PROGRESSIVE OR PRESENT PERFECT

Write questions about David Suzuki. Use the words in parentheses and the present perfect progressive or present perfect. Answer the questions with the information from Exercise 2.

1. (How many books / Suzuki / write)

   A: *How many books has Suzuki written?*

   B: *He's written more than 40 books.*

2. (he / win / any awards)

   A: _____

   B: _____

3. (How long / he / be retired)

   A: _____

   B: _____

4. (How many honorary degrees / he / receive)

   A: _____

   B: _____

5. (How long / his foundation / exist)

   A: _____

   B: _____

6. (What / the Foundation / teach / young people)

   A: _____

   B: _____

7. (What activity / Suzuki / stop)

   A: _____

   B: _____

8. (he / develop / a lot of TV shows)

   A: _____

   B: _____

(continued on next page)

9. (How long / people / watch / *The Nature of Things*)

A: _____

B: _____

10. (What / Suzuki / do / to spread his message)

A: _____

B: _____

EXERCISE 5 EDITING

Read the student's blog. There are nine mistakes in the use of the present perfect progressive and present perfect. The first mistake is already corrected. Find and correct eight more.

● ● ●

Friday, April 22 (Earth Day!)

                                                   been taking

It's the second week of the fall semester. I've ~~taken~~ a course on environmental issues with Professor McCarthy. He's an expert on the subject of global warming, and he's already been writing two books on the topic. I think one of them has even been winning an award.

For the past two weeks, we've studying pollution and how the Earth's temperature have been getting warmer. As part of the course, we've been reading a lot of books on the environment. For example, I've just been finishing a book called *The Sacred Balance: Rediscovering Our Place in Nature* by David Suzuki. He's a well-known Canadian scientist and environmentalist. It was fascinating. Since then, I've also read his autobiography. I've only been reading about 50 pages of the book so far, but it seems interesting, too. I'm really learning a lot in this course, and I've been started to change some of the things I do in order to help protect the planet.

EXERCISE 6 PERSONAL WRITING

What *have you done* or *have you been doing* lately to help the environment? Write a paragraph. Use the list in Exercise 3 on page 76 or your own ideas. Use some of the phrases from the box.

For several years, I . . .	I haven't been . . .
I have . . .	Lately, . . .
I have been . . .	Since I read about global warming, I . . .
I haven't . . .	Since 20__, . . .

EXAMPLE: Since I read about global warming, I've been trying to use less gasoline. For example, I've started . . .

_____

_____

_____

_____

_____

_____

_____

_____

_____

_____

_____

_____

_____

EXERCISE 1 AFFIRMATIVE AND NEGATIVE STATEMENTS WITH *CAN* AND *COULD*

Read about a student's ability in English. Then complete the statements for each item. (For items 8–10, write complete statements.) Use *can, can't, could,* or *couldn't*.

Student's Name _Fernando Ochoa_

English Language Ability Questionnaire

Skill	Now	Before This Course
1. understand conversational English	✔	✘
2. understand recorded announcements	✘	✘
3. read an English newspaper	✔	✔
4. read an English novel	✘	✘
5. speak on the phone	✔	✘
6. speak with a group of people	✔	✘
7. write an email	✔	✔
8. write a business letter	✘	✘
9. order a meal in English	✔	✔
10. go shopping	✔	✔

1. Before this course, he _couldn't understand conversational English_ _____.

Now he _can understand conversational English_ _____.

2. He _____ _couldn't understand recorded announcements_ _____ before the course, and

he still _can't understand recorded announcements_ _____.

3. He _____ now, and he

_____ before, too.

4. He _____ before the course, and

he still _____.

5. Now he _____ but before the course

   he _____.

6. Before the course, he _____, but

   now he _____.

7. Before the course, he _____.

   He still _____, of course.

8. _____

   _____.

9. _____

   _____.

10. _____

    _____.

11. **SUMMARY:** Fernando _____

    do a lot more now than he _____ before the course.

EXERCISE 2 QUESTIONS AND ANSWERS WITH *CAN* AND *COULD*

A reporter from the school newspaper is interviewing a new student. Use *can* or *could* and
the words in parentheses to write the interview questions and the student's answers.

1. (speak / any other languages)

   REPORTER: *Can you speak any other languages?* _____

   STUDENT: *Yes, I can.* _____ I speak two other languages.

2. (What languages / speak)

   REPORTER: _____

   STUDENT: Spanish and French.

3. (speak Spanish / when you were a child)

   REPORTER: _____

   STUDENT: _____ I learned it as an adult.

(continued on next page)

4. (speak French)

REPORTER: _____

STUDENT: _____ We spoke French some of the time at home.

5. (before you came here / understand spoken English)

REPORTER: _____

STUDENT: _____ I didn't understand anything! I was always confused. I

hated it.

6. (understand song lyrics)

REPORTER: What about now? _____

STUDENT: _____ Especially if I listen to them more than once.

7. (before this course / write a business letter in English)

REPORTER: _____

STUDENT: _____ But I used to write in English to my friends.

8. (drive a car before you came here)

REPORTER: So, tell me some more about yourself. _____

STUDENT: _____ I was too young.

9. (drive a car now)

REPORTER: _____

STUDENT: _____ I still haven't learned.

10. (swim)

REPORTER: We're not far from the beach here. _____

STUDENT: _____ I've been swimming since I was a little kid.

11. (surf before you came here)

REPORTER: What about surfing? _____

STUDENT: _____ But I learned to surf the first month I was here.

12. (What / do now / that / you / not do before)

REPORTER: _____

STUDENT: Oh, I _____ a lot of things now that I _____

before. For example, I can now have this interview with you!

EXERCISE 3 AFFIRMATIVE AND NEGATIVE: *CAN* AND *CAN'T*

Complete the article about hearing loss with *can* or *can't* and the correct words from the boxes.

damage	~~hear~~	recover	survive

Some people ___can't hear___ as a result of a childhood illness, but many people lose their
_____ 1.

hearing as a result of everyday exposure to loud noise. Very loud sounds _____ the
_____ 2.

hair cells in your ear, which are necessary for hearing. These cells _____ from mild
_____ 3.

damage, but they _____ severe damage, which kills them and causes permanent
_____ 4.

hearing loss.

be	do	leave	listen	lose	understand

Many people are exposed to loud noise at work. Construction workers, factory workers, and

firefighters are just a few examples. But did you know that you _____ your hearing
_____ 5.

from your smartphone and other personal listening devices that you use with earphones? In part

because of longer-lasting batteries, people _____ for hours without taking a break.
_____ 6.

So, what _____ YOU _____ to protect your ears? Here are a few tips.
_____ 7.

- Wear safety earmuffs or earplugs if you work in a loud environment.

- Turn the volume down on your smartphone when listening to music.

- Don't sit near the band or loudspeakers at a concert or party.

And be aware of the noise level in your environment. What's too loud? If you have to shout so

that someone near you _____ you, the noise level is dangerous. If you
_____ 8.

_____ the area, take other steps to protect your ears. When it comes to your hearing,
_____ 9.

you _____ too careful!
_____ 10.

EXERCISE 4 AFFIRMATIVE AND NEGATIVE STATEMENTS WITH *BE ABLE TO*

Read the article about hearing loss. Complete the article with the correct form of *be able to* and the verbs in parentheses.

Living in a Hearing World

There are millions of people who have some degree of hearing loss. There are two major

types of hearing loss.

1. **Sound Sensitivity Loss.** People with this kind of loss _____are not able to hear_____

   1. (not hear)

   soft sounds—a whisper or a bird singing, for example. However, when sounds are loud

   enough, they _____ them correctly.

   2. (interpret)

2. **Sound Discrimination Loss.** People with this particular kind of hearing loss

   _____ one sound from another. As a result of this,

   3. (not distinguish)

   they _____ speech—even when it is loud enough

   4. (not understand)

   for them to hear.

How do people with hearing disabilities get along in a hearing world? Most people with

hearing impairments _____ some sounds. With the use

5. (hear)

of hearing aids and cochlear implants (devices put in the ear during an operation), many

people _____ some of their ability to hear. Some people

6. (get back)

with hearing disabilities _____ lips. But, at best, lip-reading

7. (read)

is only 30 to 50 percent effective. Even a good lip-reader _____

8. (not recognize)

all the sounds. Just ask someone to silently mouth the words *pat*, *bat*, and *mat*. The three

words sound different, but they all *look* the same when someone says them. In addition, the

human eye _____ fast enough to process speech by

9. (not work)

vision alone. By far the most successful form of communication is signing—the use of sign

language. People with hearing impairments _____

10. (communicate)

successfully with others who know this language.

EXERCISE 5 QUESTIONS AND SHORT ANSWERS WITH *BE ABLE TO*

Modern technology can make life easier for people with hearing loss. Read this FAQ (frequently asked questions) page of a website about assisted-hearing devices. Use *will be able to* to complete the questions and write short answers.

Assisted-Hearing Devices: FAQs

Q: My daughter has a hearing disability. She's going to have her first child next month.

_____Will_____ she _____be able to know_____ when the baby is crying?
                                       1. (know)

A: _____Yes, she will_____. She can get a device that flashes lights (so she'll be
              2.
able to see the signal) or vibrates (so she'll be able to feel the signal).

******

Q: My nephew can't hear the alarm clock in the morning. I want to buy him a flashing

lamp. _____ he _____ it when he's sleeping?
                                3. (how / see)

A: You can see a strong light through your eyelids—as long as you don't have your head

under the covers!

******

Q: I'm thinking of getting a cochlear implant. _____ I _____
                                        4. (hear)
"normally" with it?

A: _____. Hearing with an implant is not the same as
              5.
"normal" hearing, but it can help a lot.

******

Q: I just moved into a new apartment, and I'm having trouble hearing the doorbell.

_____ I _____ this problem without disturbing
                            6. (how / solve)
my neighbors?

A: You can get a system that produces sound in different locations in your apartment—

not just at the front door.

******

(continued on next page)

Q: My husband and I both wear hearing aids, and we both love to travel. _____

we _____ the theater when we're in London next summer?

　　　　　　　　7. (enjoy)

A: _____. Theaters in London use a "loop" system. This

　　　　8.

system sends sounds directly to your hearing aid (without wires!). You just need to set

your hearing aid to "T." Have a good trip!

EXERCISE 6 CONTRAST: *CAN* AND *BE ABLE TO*

Read the article about a well-known actress who is deaf. Complete the story with the correct form of *can, could,* or *be able to* and the verbs in parentheses. Use *can* or *could* when possible.

Marlee Matlin: Actress and Activist

Actress Marlee Matlin _____*could hear*_____ at

　　　　　　　　　　　　　　　1. (hear)

birth but lost her hearing at the age of eighteen months as a result

of a childhood illness. By the age of five, young Marlee

_____ lips. Shortly after that, she

　　　　　　2. (read)

mastered sign language. At first, Matlin felt angry and frightened

by her hearing impairment. "I wanted to be perfect, and I

_____ my deafness," she said during an interview. With time,

　　　3. (not accept)

however, she learned to accept it.

Matlin began her acting career at the age of eight, when she performed in theater for the

deaf. It was clear from the start that she had a lot of talent. In 1986, she received an Oscar

award for best actress in the Hollywood film *Children of a Lesser God*. In the movie, she

played the role of an angry woman who was deaf and did not want to speak. For Matlin,

however, speaking is very important. At the Oscar ceremony, the proud actress

_____ her award verbally. It was the first time the public heard

　　　4. (accept)

her speak. "It's what I wanted to do because a lot of people all over the world

_____ me for who I am," she said. Matlin was worried, however.
5. (see)

"What other roles _____ I _____ in
6. (do)

the future?" she wanted to know.

Matlin didn't need to worry. She continued to receive important roles in movies and on

TV. Her work has helped change people's perceptions of what deaf people can and cannot

do. One reviewer said, "She _____ more saying nothing than
7. (do)

most people _____ talking." Today, thanks to intensive speech
8. (do)

training and a lot of dedication, she _____ very clearly. In 1994,
9. (speak)

she _____ something for the first time: She played the role of a
10. (achieve)

character who was not deaf. Matlin, in fact, doesn't think of herself as a "deaf actress." She's

an "actress who happens to be deaf." One of her aspirations is that in the future she

_____ more roles that are not specifically for people with hearing
11. (get)

impairments.

In addition to her acting career, Matlin is actively trying to improve lives. In 1995, she

helped get an important law passed in the United States. As a result of this law, today most

TV sets have closed-captioning on their screens so that hearing-impaired viewers

_____ everything. In 2011, she wrote letters supporting a
12. (read)

proposal to include captions in all movies shown in movie theaters. If this proposal passes,

deaf people _____ the same movies as hearing people.
13. (enjoy)

Matlin does not believe in limits. "I _____ attitudes on
14. (change)

deafness and prove we _____ everything—except hear," she said.
15. (do)

EXERCISE 7 EDITING

Read the student's composition. There are nine mistakes in the use of *can, could,* and *be able to*. The first one is already corrected. Find and correct eight more.

>   *couldn't*
>   Before I came to this country, I ~~can't~~ do many things in English. For example,
> I couldn't follow a conversation if many people were talking at the same time.
> I always got confused. I remember a party I went to. Everyone was speaking
> English, and I wasn't able understand a word! I felt so uncomfortable. Finally, my
> aunt came to pick me up, and I could leave the party.
>
>   Today, I can to understand much better. I am taking classes at the adult center.
> My teacher is very good. She can explains things well, and she always gives us
> the chance to talk a lot in class. When I finish this class in May, I can speak and
> understand a lot better.
>
>   Speaking English well is very important to me. I practice a lot at home, too.
> When I first came to this country, I can't understand very much TV, but now I can
> to understand much better. In fact, I can do a lot now, and I think in a few more
> months I can do even more.

EXERCISE 8 PERSONAL WRITING

Look at the English Language Ability Questionnaire in Exercise 1 on page 80. Write a paragraph about your English ability now and before this course. Use *can, can't, could, couldn't,* and *be able to.*

EXAMPLE: My English has improved quite a lot. Before I started studying here, I couldn't understand conversational English very much at all, but now I'm able to understand a lot more. For example, I can . . .

_____

_____

_____

_____

_____

_____

_____

_____

_____

_____

_____

_____

_____

Permission: *Can, Could, May, Do you mind if*

EXERCISE 1 QUESTIONS AND RESPONSES

Match the classroom questions and responses.

Questions

_d_	**1.**	Do you mind if I bring my friends to class?
___	**2.**	May I ask a question?
___	**3.**	Do you mind if I record the class?
___	**4.**	Could I open the window?
___	**5.**	Can we review Unit 4?
___	**6.**	May I leave the room?
___	**7.**	Could we use our dictionaries?
___	**8.**	Could I borrow a pen?

Responses

a. Certainly. The key to the restroom is hanging on the wall.

b. Not at all. I think it's a good idea.

c. Sure. I hope I can answer it.

d. Sorry. It's already pretty crowded.

e. Sure. But remember: You don't have to look up every word.

f. I'm afraid we can't. We're out of time.

g. Sure. But please remember to return it.

h. Go right ahead. It's quite warm in here.

EXERCISE 2 QUESTIONS

Read the classroom situations. Complete the questions asking for permission.

1. You want to open the window.

   May *I open the window?* _____

2. Your whole class wants to review Unit 6.

   Could _____

3. You want to borrow a classmate's pen.

   Can _____

4. You want to look at someone's class notes.

   Do you mind if _____

5. You want to come late to the next class.

   Do you mind if _____

6. Your roommate wants to come to the next class with you.

   Could _____

7. You want to ask a question.

May _____

8. You and a classmate would like to use a dictionary.

Can _____

9. You and your classmates want to leave five minutes early.

Could _____

10. Your sister wants to go on the class trip with the rest of the class.

Do you mind if _____

EXERCISE 3 AFFIRMATIVE AND NEGATIVE STATEMENTS

Look at the flyer. Complete the statements with the words in parentheses.

Class Trip
You are invited to our annual class picnic on
Sunday, May 26, at Glenwood State Park.
Food and beverages welcome, but no glass containers, please!
Bus tickets $5.00 (check or cash)
Advance purchase only • No refunds
Bring a friend!
Don't forget your bathing suit! The lake is beautiful.

1. You _____ *may bring* _____ a friend.
(may / bring)

2. You _____ your own food.
(can / bring)

3. You _____ your own drinks.
(can / bring)

4. You _____ juice from a glass bottle at the picnic.
(can / drink)

5. You _____ for your bus ticket by check.
(can / pay)

6. You _____ for your bus ticket with cash.
(can / pay)

7. You _____ for your ticket with a credit card.
(may / pay)

8. You _____ your bus ticket on the day of the trip.
(may / purchase)

9. You _____ a refund.
(can / get)

10. You _____ in the lake.
(may / swim)

EXERCISE 4 EDITING

Read the professor's response to an email from one of his students. (The professor's answers are in **bold print**.) There are six mistakes in making and responding to requests. The first one is already corrected. Find and correct five more.

Subject: Missed classes—Reply
Date: 04-23-16 11:22:43 EST
From: profwilson@bryant.edu
To: Timbotwo@hotline.com

Professor Wilson—

I've been sick for the past two days. That's why I missed the last test. I'm really annoyed.
                                                                    take
I studied a lot for it and was really well prepared. May I ~~taking~~ a make-up exam?

I know you never miss class, Tim, so I assumed that's what happened. I hope you're

feeling better. Yes, you can take a make-up exam if you bring a doctor's note.

If I can take the exam, may I use my calculator during the test?

No, you mayn't! It's against the guidelines we established at the beginning of the

semester. Remember?

Could my roommate comes to class and take notes for me on Thursday?

Yes, he could. I hope you can read his handwriting!

Do you mind when he records Allison's presentation for me? I don't want to miss it.

Not at all. It's fine for him to record the presentation.

One last thing—I know I missed some handouts. May I have please copies of them?

Sure. I'll give them to your roommate on Thursday.

Thanks a lot.

Tim

EXERCISE 5 PERSONAL WRITING

Write an email to your teacher asking for permission to do something. Use at least two situations (from the box or your own ideas). Use *can I, could I, may I,* or *do you mind if.*

> You've been having difficulty understanding what the teacher is saying.
> You're feeling sick and need to miss class.
> Your cousin (from your country) is going to visit you for a week.
> You're having trouble with a paper you're writing.
> You'd like to use your calculator during your math test.

EXAMPLE: Dear Ms. Johnson,

I'm not feeling well, and I'm going to have to miss our next class. I know you're giving a test that day. Could I take the test next week instead of on Wednesday? Also, at the end of the month, my cousin...

_____

_____

_____

_____

_____

_____

_____

_____

_____

_____

_____

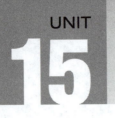
Requests: *Can, Could, Will, Would, Would you mind*

EXERCISE 1 REQUESTS AND RESPONSES

Match the office requests and responses.

Requests

<u>d</u>   **1.** Could you meet me tomorrow at 8:00 a.m.?

_____ **2.** Will you please type this memo for me?

_____ **3.** Could you show me how to use the scanner?

_____ **4.** Would you please spell your last name for me?

_____ **5.** Would you mind distributing this report for me?

_____ **6.** Can you cancel tomorrow's meeting for me? I have to go out of town.

_____ **7.** Will you shut the window, please?

_____ **8.** Would you get that box down from the closet? I'd really appreciate it.

_____ **9.** Could you get the phone for me?

_____ **10.** Can you give me Doug Johnson's email address?

Responses

a. I'd be glad to. When do you need it?

b. Sure. It is pretty cold in here.

c. Of course I can. When would you like to reschedule it?

d. I'm sorry. I have an early-morning dentist appointment.

e. Sure. It's Djohn@iol.com.

f. Sure. . . . Hello, J & R Equities.

g. Sure. It's M-A-R-D-J-A-I-T.

h. Sorry, but I don't know how. Ask Todd. He knows how.

i. I'd like to, but it's too heavy for me to lift.

j. Not at all.

Write the letters of the responses that mean "Yes": <u>a</u>_____

Write the letters of the responses that mean "No": _____

Write the letter of the response that has a negative word, but means "OK, I'll do it.":

_____

EXERCISE 2 REQUESTS

These conversations take place in an office. Use the correct form of the phrases from the box to complete the requests.

~~answer the phone~~	keep the noise down
buy some stamps	lend me $5.00
come to my office	open the window
explain this note to me	pick up a sandwich
get Frank's phone number	stay late tonight

1. **A:** Could you _____*answer the phone*_____? My hands are full.

   B: Sure. I'll get it.

2. **A:** Would you mind _____? It's really hot in here.

   B: No, not at all.

3. **A:** Can you please _____ for me?

   B: Certainly. I pass the post office on my way home.

4. **A:** I'm going to the coffee shop. Can I get you anything?

   B: Could you _____ for me?

5. **A:** Would you mind _____? We really have to get this report done by tomorrow.

   B: I'm sorry, but I have to visit my aunt in the hospital.

6. **A:** Will you _____, please? I can't hear myself think!

   B: Sorry!

7. **A:** Can you _____ when you have the chance?

   B: Sure. I'll be right there.

8. **A:** Would you _____ for me?

   B: It's 555–4345.

9. **A:** Would you mind _____?

   B: Not at all. What don't you understand?

10. **A:** Could you _____?

    B: Oh, I'm sorry. I'm short on cash.

EXERCISE 3 WORD ORDER

Unscramble the words to make requests. Use the correct form of the verbs.

1. come / can / please / here / you

   <u>Can you please come here?</u> OR <u>Can you come here, please?</u>

2. work / on Saturday / would you mind

   _____

3. you / me / please / will / help

   _____

4. would / please / text / you / your decision / me

   _____

5. drive / home / you / me / please / could

   _____

EXERCISE 4 EDITING

Read the office messages. There are six mistakes in making requests. The first mistake is already corrected. Find and correct five more. Don't forget to check punctuation.

1.

Meng,
Would you ~~filed~~ file these, please?
Thanks,
R. L.

2.

write it down

Hi Ted,
   Could you please remember to turn off the lights when you leave?
Thanks,
Lynn

3.

HANK,

WILL YOU RETURN PLEASE THE STAPLER?

BRAD

4.

Melinda,

Can you make 5 copies of these pages, please?

Thanks,

Ellen

5.

John,

Would you mind deliver the finished report to me before you leave for the day?

Rey

6.

Celia,
Could you please remember to lock the door.
Thank you.

Diana

7.

Annie,
Would you please to call Ms. Rivera before the end of the day?

thanks,

JF

8.

Todd—
Could you print out 10 copies of the Hendricks report?
Also, would you mind to email Lisa Barker a copy? That'll cheer her up!

Thanks a lot.
Heather

EXERCISE 5 PERSONAL WRITING

Write a note to someone you live with. Make at least three requests with *can, could, will, would,* or *would you mind.* Use some of the situations from the box or your own ideas.

the building manager has called twice	the living room is messy
the dishes are dirty	the plants need watering
the electric bill hasn't been paid	the refrigerator is almost empty

EXAMPLE: Hi Brian,

I've got to leave for school now and I won't be back until after 8:00 tonight. Could you please wash the dishes? Also, the refrigerator is almost empty. We need some food in the house. Would you . . . ?

_____

_____

_____

_____

_____

_____

_____

_____

_____

_____

_____

16 Advice: *Should, Ought to, Had better*

EXERCISE 1 AFFIRMATIVE AND NEGATIVE STATEMENTS WITH *SHOULD*

Rewrite the cell-phone tips. Give advice with *should.* Choose between affirmative and negative.

CELL-PHONE ETIQUETTE

Cell phones have made communication a lot easier, but they can also be very annoying. Here are some rules you should follow to be polite.

- Turn off your cell phone in public places such as movie theaters and class.

  1. You should turn off your cell phone in public places such as movie theaters and class.

- Don't shout into the phone.

  2. _____

- Speak in a quiet, normal voice.

  3. _____

- Leave the room to make a phone call.

  4. _____

- Don't discuss private issues in public places. Protect your own and other people's privacy.

  5. _____

- Don't stand too close to other people when you are talking on the phone.

  6. _____

- Pay attention to other people on the street when you are walking and talking.

  7. _____

- Never use a cell phone when you are driving. Even hands-free phones are dangerous.

  8. _____

EXERCISE 2 AFFIRMATIVE AND NEGATIVE STATEMENTS WITH *SHOULD, OUGHT TO, HAD BETTER*

Complete the conversations with the correct form of the verbs in parentheses. Choose between affirmative and negative. Use contractions when possible.

1. **A:** Excuse me, but you really ____*shouldn't use*____ your cell phone in here. The sign says, "No
(should / use)

   cell phones."

   B: Sorry. I didn't see the sign.

2. **A:** You _____ Aunt Rosa. I know she'd be happy to hear from you.
(should / call)

   B: Good idea. I'll call her as soon as I get off the phone with you.

3. **A:** You _____ to pick up some milk on the way home. We're all out of it, and we
(had better / forget)

   need it for dinner.

   B: Call me again to remind me. OK?

4. **A:** We _____ the movie at Cinemax Saturday night. I hear it's really great.
(ought to / see)

   B: OK. But we _____ tickets in the afternoon, or it'll be hard to get a seat.
(had better / buy)

   A: Maybe we _____ them online. That way we can avoid standing in line! I just
(should / get)

   hate waiting in line.

5. **A:** We _____ that restaurant near the theater.
(should / try)

   B: Good idea. I'll call and make a reservation.

6. **A:** Our cell phone bill is really high. I think we _____ about changing plans.
(ought to / think)

   B: You're right. We _____ it.
(should / look into)

7. **A:** People really _____ on their cell phones while they're driving. It's very
(should / talk)

   dangerous behavior.

   B: You know, it's illegal in many places.

   A: Well, there _____ a law against it here, too.
(should / be)

8. **A:** You _____ Andy now. He's probably already asleep.
(had better / call)

   B: OK. I'll call him tomorrow.

9. **A:** They _____ a "quiet car" on this train. It's hard to work with all these people
(ought to / have)

   talking on their cell phones.

   B: That's a great idea.

10. A: I _____ call-waiting on my cell phone. I'm missing too many calls without it.
(should / get)

   B: I'm surprised you don't have it already.

11. A: I _____ caller ID, too.
(ought to / have)

   B: Absolutely. It's important to know the identity of the person calling you.

12. A: I _____ so loud. I think I'm disturbing people around me.
(should / talk)

   B: Just call me when you get home. OK?

13. A: It's 7:00. I _____ now. I don't want to be late.
(had better / hang up)

   B: OK. Talk to you later.

EXERCISE 3 QUESTIONS AND ANSWERS WITH *SHOULD*

Read the invitation. Use the words in parentheses and the information in the invitation to complete the phone conversation.

YOU ARE INVITED TO A PARTY!

FOR: Scott's SURPRISE birthday barbecue

DATE: June 11

TIME: 2:00 p.m. sharp!

PLACE: 20 Greenport Avenue

RSVP by May 15. Please don't call here!
Call Amy's cell phone and leave a message.
500-555-3234
No gifts, please!
(but please bring something to drink)

LISA: Hi, Tania.

TANIA: Hi, Lisa. What's up?

LISA: Aunt Rosa's having a birthday party for Uncle Scott. She didn't have your new address,

so she asked me to call and invite you. It's on June 11. Can you come?

TANIA: Sure. Just give me all the information. (What time / be there)

What time should I be there?
—————————————————————————————————
1.

(continued on next page)

LISA: Let's see. I have the invitation right here.

You should be there at 2:00 p.m. sharp.
_____
2.

TANIA: (What / wear)

_____
3.

LISA: Something casual. It's a barbecue.

TANIA: (bring a gift)

_____
4.

LISA: _____ The invitation says, "No gifts."
5.

TANIA: OK. What about food? (bring something to eat or drink)

_____
6.

LISA: _____
7.

Oh, and the invitation says, "RSVP." In other words, Aunt Rosa wants a response.

TANIA: (When / respond)

_____
8.

LISA: _____
9.

TANIA: (call Aunt Rosa)

_____
10.

LISA: _____ I forgot to tell you. It's a _surprise_ party!
11.

TANIA: OK. (Who / call)

_____
12.

LISA: _____
13.

TANIA: Fine. Sounds like fun. I'll see you there. Thanks for calling.

LISA: No problem. See you there.

EXERCISE 4 EDITING

Read the quiz. There are eleven mistakes in the use of *should, ought to,* and *had better.*
The first mistake is already corrected. Find and correct ten more.

Party Etiquette Quiz

Do you know what you should do at a party? Check (✔) the best answer.

1. You are at a party and you can't remember someone's name. What ~~you should~~ ^{should you} do?

   ☐ a. You should no ask the person's name.

   ☐ b. You better avoid the person or leave immediately

   ☐ c. You ought just ask.

2. You don't know anyone at the party, and your host doesn't introduce you to the

   other guests. Had you better introduce yourself?

   ☐ a. Yes, you should. You should say, "Hi. My name's _____."

   ☐ b. No, you should. You'd better tell the host to introduce you.

3. Your cell phone rings during the party. You should answer it?

   ☐ a. Just let it ring. You had not better answer it.

   ☐ b. You should answer it, but just have a short conversation.

   ☐ c. You really ought to leave the room and speak to the person in private.

4. You had a very nice time at the party. How you should thank your host?

   ☐ a. You should just say "thank you" when you leave.

   ☐ b. You should send a "thank-you" email the next day.

   ☐ c. You oughta write a long "thank-you" letter and send a gift, too.

5. Everyone brought gifts to the party. You didn't.

   ☐ a. You'd better to apologize right away.

   ☐ b. You shouldn't say anything, but you ought to send a gift later.

   ☐ c. You should leave immediately and go buy a gift.

EXERCISE 5 PERSONAL WRITING

Imagine that a friend of yours is going to a party. He or she won't know anyone there and feels a little nervous. Write an email giving your friend advice. Use some of the phrases from the box.

You really should . . .	You shouldn't . . .
You ought to . . .	You'd better not . . .
You'd better . . .	Maybe you should . . .

EXAMPLE: Hi Hannah,

Stop worrying! I'm sure you'll have a good time at the party. I think you should just relax and try to be yourself. Before you go, you ought to . . .

_____

_____

_____

_____

_____

_____

_____

_____

_____

_____

UNIT

17

Nouns and Quantifiers

EXERCISE 1 NOUNS

A. Read the article about an ancient Egyptian king. Underline the nouns.

TUT'S TOMB[1]: AN EGYPTIAN TIME CAPSULE

Tutankhamun, better known as King Tut, became king of ancient Egypt when he was only nine years old. He died before his nineteenth birthday around 1323 B.C.E., and was mostly forgotten. Thousands of years later, British archaeologist Howard Carter searched for his tomb. In 1922, after searching for many years, he finally found it near the Nile River, across from the modern Egyptian city of Luxor. Inside he discovered thousands of items buried along with the young king. Among the many treasures[2] were:

- furniture—including couches and chairs
- jewelry—including bracelets and necklaces
- clothing—including gloves, scarves, and shoes
- musical instruments
- chariots[3]
- vases and jars
- pots made of clay[4] (they probably once contained money)
- games and toys (Tut played with them as a child)
- food and wine
- gold

Tut's tomb is a time capsule. It gives us a picture of how Egyptian kings lived more than 3000 years ago, how they died, and what they expected to need in their lives after death.

Since his discovery, Tut has not been resting in peace. He and his treasures have traveled to exhibitions around the world, where millions of visitors have been able to view some of the wonders[5] of his ancient civilization.

[1] **tomb:** a place where a dead body is buried; ancient Egyptian kings' tombs were very large and often had several rooms
[2] **treasures:** valuable and important objects such as gold and jewelry
[3] **chariots:** ancient forms of transportation made of wood with two wheels and pulled by a horse
[4] **clay:** heavy soil that is soft when wet, but hard when dry or baked
[5] **wonders:** amazing things

B. Put the nouns from the article into the correct columns. Choose only sixteen count nouns.

Proper Nouns	Common Nouns			
	Count Nouns		Non-Count Nouns	
1. _____Tut_____	1. _____tomb_____	9. _____	1. __furniture__	6. _____
2. _____	2. _____	10. _____	2. _____	7. _____
3. _____	3. _____	11. _____	3. _____	8. _____
4. _____	4. _____	12. _____	4. _____	9. _____
5. _____	5. _____	13. _____	5. _____	10. _____
6. _____	6. _____	14. _____		
7. _____	7. _____	15. _____		
	8. _____	16. _____		

EXERCISE 2 NOUN AND VERB AGREEMENT

Complete the fact sheet with the correct form of the words in parentheses.

Did You Know . . . ?

The Pyramids

▲ Egypt's official _____name is_____ the Arab Republic
    1. (name / be)
of Egypt.

▲ The _____ in northeastern Africa and
    2. (country / lie)
southwestern Asia.

▲ About 20 million _____ in the Greater Cairo area. Cairo is the capital of Egypt.
    3. (people / live)

▲ _____ many interesting sites for tourists to visit, including many pyramids.
    4. (Cairo / have)

▲ _____ one of the most important export crops. _____ in
    5. (cotton / be)   **6. (rice / grow)**
many parts of the country and is an important food crop.

▲ Most _____ Egypt during the months of October through May.
    7. (tourist / visit)

▲ The Islamic holy month of _____ for one month at a different
    8. (Ramadan / take place)
time each year. During Ramadan many _____.
    9. (shop and restaurant / close)

▲ The _____ usually very hot in the summer. Cool, comfortable
    10. (weather / be)
_____ important, and _____ a must.
  11. (clothing / be)   **12. (sunhat / be)**

EXERCISE 3 QUANTIFIERS

Circle the correct words to complete this FAQ about traveling to Egypt.

Q: How many / (much) time should I spend in Cairo?
1.

A: There are so many / much things to do and see in this great city that you could easily
2.

spend a great deal of / several weeks there. Most people can't, though, so we
3.

recommend at least a little / a few days.
4.

Q: Do many / much people speak English?
5.

A: Yes. Arabic is the official language, but few / a lot of people speak English.
6.

Q: How many / much money should I take?
7.

A: In the big cities, many / few places accept credit cards, so you don't need to carry
8.

a little / much cash. There are also ATMs. But in smaller places, it's a good idea to
9.

have some / several cash or traveler's checks.
10.

Q: I'm thinking about renting a car. Is it easy to get around?

A: It's not a great idea to drive, especially in the cities. There is a lot of / several traffic.
11.

In the city, use a taxi. Cairo has a subway, too.

Q: I'd like to go on a Nile River cruise. Can I book that once I'm in Egypt?

A: Yes. There are a few / few travel agencies in Cairo and Luxor that arrange tours that
12.

include boat trips.

Q: I'll need to buy any / some souvenirs to bring home. What do you recommend?
13.

A: You have little / a lot of great choices. It's always nice to bring back some / a few
14.   15.

gold or silver jewelry. You'll also find some / several beautiful cotton fabric. And don't
16.

forget to pick up some / any spices at one of the enough / many markets you'll see.
17.   18.

Q: This may seem like a strange question, but how did King Tut die?

A: Many / Much people ask that! For many / much years, historians believed Tut was
19.   20.

killed. Today, there is several / a lot of evidence that he died as a result of a disease
21.

and severe injuries to his leg.

EXERCISE 4 EDITING

Read the posts to a travel website. There are sixteen mistakes in the use of nouns, verb and pronoun agreement, and quantifiers. The first mistake is already corrected. Find and correct fifteen more.

                                              Egypt
I can't tell you how much we enjoyed our trip to ~~egypt~~. We just returned few days ago. What an

amazing country! There are so much things to see and do. My only complaint are that we didn't

have enough time! But, we'll be back!

Hans Koch, Germany

We saw a lot of tombs and pyramids on our recent trip, but the best were the three Giza pyramids.

It is huge! And, I was surprised to learn, they are located right at the edge of the city of Cairo.

Because of this, there is a lot of traffic getting there (and back). There were also a lot tourists.

The day we were there it was very hot. If you go, you should know that there are a few places to

get anything to drink, so I REALLY recommend that you bring any water with you. Oh, and if

you want to see the inside of a pyramid, you need a special ticket, and they only sell a little

tickets each day. Get there early if you want one!

Vilma Ortiz, USA

The food are great in Egypt! We went to some wonderful Restaurants. We found out about one

place near our hotel that doesn't have much tourists. Mostly local people eats there and everyone

was really friendly. I particularly enjoyed the "meze" (a variety of appetizers). You choose a little

different plates before you order your main dish. Delicious!

Jim Cook, England

There are many beautiful beach in Alexandria. A lot of them are private or connected to hotels,

but there are also public ones, so be sure to bring a bathing suit if you visit that part of Egypt. The

water were warm—I felt like in a bathtub!

Aki Kato, Japan

EXERCISE 5 PERSONAL WRITING

Imagine that you just came back from a trip. Write an email to a friend about the trip. Use some of the phrases from the box and ideas of your own.

I really liked . . .	The people . . .
I saw . . .	The weather . . .
The buildings . . .	There were . . .
The food . . .	We bought . . .

EXAMPLE: Hi! I just got back from Lima, Peru! It's a really interesting city. The people are very friendly and . . .

_____

_____

_____

_____

_____

_____

_____

_____

_____

_____

_____

_____

Articles: Indefinite and Definite

EXERCISE 1 INDEFINITE AND DEFINITE ARTICLES

Some people are talking in school. Circle the correct words to complete the conversations.
If you don't need an article, circle Ø.

1. **A:** Can I borrow a / the pen?

   B: Sure. Take a / the one on a / the desk. I don't need it.

2. **A:** Is a / the teacher here yet?

   B: No, she hasn't come yet.

3. **A:** What do you think of Mr. Jackson?

   B: He's wonderful. He's a / the best teacher I've ever had.

4. **A:** Have you done the / Ø homework?

   B: Yes. But I don't think I got a / the last answer right.

5. **A:** Could you open a / the window, please?

   B: Which one?

   A: A / The one next to a / the door.

6. **A:** Who's that?

   B: That's a / the school principal.

   A: Oh, I've never seen her before.

7. **A:** Do you like the / Ø history?

   B: It's OK. But I prefer the / Ø science. What about you?

   A: I'm very interested in a / the history of the / Ø ancient Greece.

8. **A:** We learned about an / the ozone layer in science class yesterday.

   B: Did you know there's an / the enormous "hole" in it?

   A: Yeah. It's pretty scary.

   B: It sure is. It was a / the first time I'd heard about it.

9. A: What kind of work do you do?

    B: I'm <u>an / the</u> engineer. What about you?

    A: I'm <u>a / Ø</u> mechanic.

10. A: Are they <u>some / Ø</u> students?

    B: I don't think so. They look like <u>the / Ø</u> teachers.

11. A: Do you know where I can get <u>some / the</u> water around here?

    B: Sure. There's <u>a / the</u> water fountain right across <u>a / the</u> hall, right next to <u>the / Ø</u> restrooms.

12. A: Do you know what <u>a / the</u> homework is for tomorrow?

    B: We have to read <u>a / the</u> fable.

    A: Which one?

    B: <u>A / The</u> one on page 23.

EXERCISE 2 INDEFINITE AND DEFINITE ARTICLES

Complete the conversation. Use *a, an,* or *the* where necessary. Use a hyphen ("-") if you don't need an article.

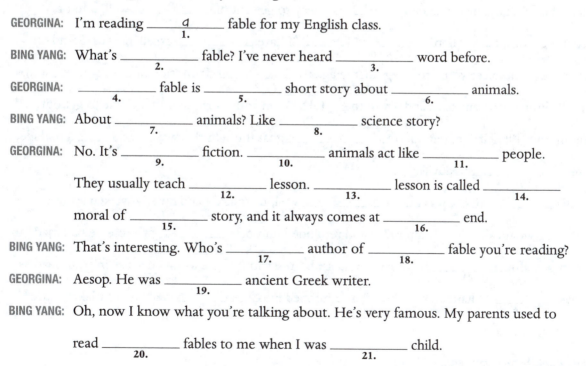

BING YANG: Hi, Georgina. What are you doing?

GEORGINA: I'm reading _____*a*_____ fable for my English class.
                 1.

BING YANG: What's _____ fable? I've never heard _____ word before.
              2.   **3.**

GEORGINA: _____ fable is _____ short story about _____ animals.
       4.   **5.**   **6.**

BING YANG: About _____ animals? Like _____ science story?
             7.   **8.**

GEORGINA: No. It's _____ fiction. _____ animals act like _____ people.
            9.   **10.**   **11.**

    They usually teach _____ lesson. _____ lesson is called _____
                   12.   **13.**   **14.**

    moral of _____ story, and it always comes at _____ end.
            15.   **16.**

BING YANG: That's interesting. Who's _____ author of _____ fable you're reading?
                          17.   **18.**

GEORGINA: Aesop. He was _____ ancient Greek writer.
               19.

BING YANG: Oh, now I know what you're talking about. He's very famous. My parents used to

    read _____ fables to me when I was _____ child.
         20.   **21.**

(continued on next page)

GEORGINA: Well, they're also good for _____ adults. I'll lend you _____ book
                                              22.   **23.**

when I'm finished if you're interested.

BING YANG: Thanks. I am.

EXERCISE 3 INDEFINITE AND DEFINITE ARTICLES

Complete this version of a famous Aesop fable. Use *a*, *an*, or *the* where necessary. Use a
hyphen ("-") if you don't need an article.

The Fox and the Goat

____A____ fox fell into _____ well. He
  1.   **2.**
struggled, but he couldn't get out again. Finally,

_____ thirsty goat came by and saw _____
  3.   **4.**
fox in _____ well. "Is _____ water good?"
       5.   **6.**

_____ goat asked. "Good?" asked _____
  7.   **8.**
fox. "It's _____ best water I've ever tasted in my
      9.

whole life. Why don't you come down and try it?"

_____ goat was very thirsty, so he immediately jumped into _____ well. When he
  10.   **11.**

was finished drinking, he looked for _____ way to get out of _____ well, but, of
               12.   **13.**

course, there wasn't any. Then _____ fox said, "I have _____ excellent idea. Stand on
                 14.   **15.**

your back legs and place your front legs firmly against _____ front side of _____ well.
                             16.   **17.**

Then, I'll climb onto your back and, from there, I'll step on your horns and I'll be able to get out.

When I'm out, I'll help you get out, too." _____ goat thought this was _____ good idea
                      18.   **19.**

and followed _____ advice.
     20.

When _____ fox was out of _____ well, he quickly and quietly walked away.
    21.   **22.**

_____ goat called loudly after him and reminded him of _____ promise he had made to
 23.   **24.**

help him out. But _____ fox turned and said, "You should have as much sense in your head as
          25.

you have _____ hairs in your beard. You jumped into _____ well before making sure
      26.   **27.**

you could get out again."

Moral: *Look before you leap.*

EXERCISE 4 EDITING

Read the student's essay. There are twelve mistakes in the use of articles. The first mistake is already corrected. Find and correct eleven more.

THE FOX

            a

A fox is ~~the~~ member of the dog family. It looks like the small, thin dog with an bushy tail, a long nose, and pointed ears. You can find the foxes in most parts of a world. Animal moves very fast, and it is the very good hunter. It eats mostly mice, but it also eats the birds, insects, rabbits, and fruit.

    Unfortunately, a people hunt foxes for their beautiful fur. They also hunt them for another reason. The fox is a intelligent, clever animal, and this makes it hard to catch. As a result, the hunters find it exciting to try to catch one. It is also because of its cleverness that a fox often appears in fables, such as a fable we just read in class.

EXERCISE 5 PERSONAL WRITING

Write one or two paragraphs about the fable in Exercise 3 on page 112. Did you like it? Why or why not? What is the meaning of the moral? Give an example of the importance of the moral in your own life. Use some of the phrases from the box.

I once had an experience . . .	The experience taught me . . .
I think it means . . .	The fable is about . . .
I think the fable is very . . .	The moral of the fable is . . .

EXAMPLE: I just read the fable called "The Fox and the Goat." The fable is about a fox that . . .

_____

_____

_____

_____

_____

_____

_____

_____

_____

_____

_____

EXERCISE 1 SPELLING

Write the adjectives and adverbs.

Adjectives	Adverbs
1. quick	*quickly*
2. *nice*	nicely
3. fast	_____
4. good	_____
5. _____	dangerously
6. beautiful	_____
7. _____	hard
8. safe	_____
9. _____	ideally
10. _____	happily
11. _____	suddenly
12. peaceful	_____
13. angry	_____
14. _____	conveniently
15. bad	_____
16. _____	thoughtfully
17. _____	hungrily
18. extreme	_____

EXERCISE 2 WORD ORDER: ADJECTIVES AND ADVERBS

Emily is telling her friend about her new apartment. Unscramble the words to complete the conversation.

ANNA: Congratulations! *I heard about your new apartment* _____.
1. (heard about / I / apartment / new / your)

EMILY: Thank you! _____!
2. (news / good / fast / travels)

ANNA: What's it like?

EMILY: _____,
3. (five / rooms / has / it / large)

_____,
4. (building / it's / large / a / very / in)

and _____.
5. (sunny / it's / very)

_____.
6. (really / we're / with it / satisfied)

ANNA: Well, it sounds ideal. How's the rent?

EMILY: _____.
7. (too / it's / bad / not)

ANNA: And what about the neighborhood?

EMILY: _____.
8. (seems / quite / it / pretty)

The landlord is a bit of a problem, though. He's friendly and very charming, but

_____.
9. (he / very / speaks / loudly)

ANNA: How come?

EMILY: _____.
10. (well / doesn't / he / hear)

ANNA: I guess nothing's perfect. I know you were looking for a long time.

_____?
11. (it / decision / was / hard / a)

EMILY: No. Not really. We really liked the apartment a lot, and it's located near school.

Besides, _____.
12. (quickly / had to / we / decide)

There were a lot of other people interested in it.

ANNA: Oh, no! Look at the time! _____.
13. (I / leave / now / have to)

_____!
14. (luck / with / good / apartment / new / your)

EMILY: Thanks. See you soon.

EXERCISE 3 ADJECTIVE OR ADVERB

Emily sent an email to a friend. Complete the email with the correct form of the words in parentheses.

Hi Lauren,

I'm _____totally_____ exhausted! James and I finished moving into our new apartment
    1. (total)
today. It was a lot of _____ work, but everything worked out _____
                        2. (hard)   **3.** (real)
_____.
4. (good)

The apartment looks very _____. It's _____ _____. The
                          5. (nice)   **6.** (extreme)   **7.** (comfortable)
only problem is with the heat. I always feel _____. We'll have to speak to the
                                              8. (cold)
landlord about it. He seems _____ _____.
                            9. (pretty) **10.** (friendly)

People tell me that the neighborhood is very _____. That's _____
                                             11. (safe)   **12.** (real)
_____ because, as you know, I get home pretty _____ from work.
13. (important)   **14.** (late)
I hate it when the streets are _____ _____ like they were in our old
                               15. (complete) **16.** (empty)
neighborhood.

Shopping is very _____, too. We can get to all the stores very _____.
                 17. (good)   **18.** (easy)
The bus stop is located _____ the apartment, and all of the buses run
                        19. (near)
_____. Everything is _____ and _____.
20. (frequent)   **21.** (nice)   **22.** (convenient)

Why don't you come for a visit? It would be _____ to see you.
                                            23. (wonderful)

Love,

Emily

P.S. I almost _____ forgot to tell you! James got a _____ job as
              24. (complete)   **25.** (new)
a computer programmer. He feels _____ _____ about it, and that,
                                26. (real) **27.** (happy)
of course, makes me _____ too.
                    28. (happy)

EXERCISE 4 *-ED* OR *-ING* ADJECTIVES

Emily and James like old movies. They are deciding which ones to watch. Circle the correct adjective forms to complete these brief movie reviews.

At Home at the Movies

BILLY BUDD Based on Herman Melville's powerful and (**1.** fascinated / (fascinating)) novel, this well-acted, well-produced film will leave you (**2.** disturbed / disturbing).

THE BURNING There's nothing at all (**3.** entertained / entertaining) about this 1981 horror film that takes place in a summer camp. You'll be (**4.** disgusted / disgusting) by all the blood in this story of revenge.

CHARIOTS OF FIRE Made in England, this is an (**5.** inspired / inspiring) story about two Olympic runners. Wonderfully acted.

COMING HOME Jon Voight plays the role of a (**6.** paralyzed / paralyzing) war veteran in this (**7.** moved / moving) drama about the effects of war. Powerful.

THE COMPETITION Well-acted love story about two pianists who fall in love while competing for the top prize in a music competition. You'll be (**8.** moved / moving). Beautiful music.

FOLLOW ME QUIETLY An extraordinarily (**9.** frightened / frightening) thriller about a mentally (**10.** disturbed / disturbing) man who kills people when it rains. Not for the weak-hearted.

THE GRADUATE Director Mike Nichols won an Academy Award for this funny but (**11.** touched / touching) look at a young man trying to figure out his life after college.

THE GREEN WALL Mario Robles Godoy's photography is absolutely (**12.** astonished / astonishing) in this story of a young Peruvian family. In Spanish with English subtitles.

INVASION OF THE BODY SNATCHERS One of the most (**13.** frightened / frightening) science-fiction movies ever made. You won't be (**14.** bored / boring).

WEST SIDE STORY No matter how many times you see this classic musical, you will never be (**15.** disappointed / disappointing). The story, based on Shakespeare's *Romeo and Juliet,* is (**16.** touched / touching), and the music by Leonard Bernstein is delightful and (**17.** excited / exciting).

WILBUR AND ORVILLE: THE FIRST TO FLY This is an exceptionally (**18.** entertained / entertaining) biography of the two famous Wright brothers. Good for kids, too. They'll learn a lot without ever being (**19.** bored / boring).

EXERCISE 5 WORD ORDER: ADJECTIVES + NOUN

Complete the sentences with the correct order of the words in parentheses.

1. Last night, we watched two _____*funny old movies*_____ starring Claudio Reggiano.
   (old / funny / movies)

2. He's a(n) _____.
   (handsome / actor / tall / Italian)

3. The movie looked great on my friend's _____.
   (new / TV / large)

4. My friend served some _____.
   (delicious / pizza / mushroom / fresh)

5. We ate it on her _____.
   (leather / comfortable / black / sofa)

6. She just moved into this _____ near the college.
   (nice / apartment / small / student)

7. It's in a _____.
   (residential / quiet / neighborhood)

8. I had a very _____.
   (evening / enjoyable / relaxing)

9. I would like to find a(n) _____ like hers.
   (small / comfortable / apartment / affordable)

EXERCISE 6 EDITING

Read the ad for an apartment. There are ten mistakes in the use of adjectives and adverbs. The first one is already corrected. Find and correct nine more.

━ FOR RENT ━

Charming
~~Charmingly~~, one-bedroom apartment in a residential peaceful neighborhood.

Convenient located near shopping, transportation, entertainment, and more.

- affordable rent

- all-new appliances

- French antique beautiful desk

- friendly neighbors

- clean and safely neighborhood

- closely to park

- quiet building

This great apartment is ideal for students, and it's immediate available.

Call 444–HOME for an appointment. You won't be disappointing! But act fastly!

This apartment amazing won't last long.

EXERCISE 7 PERSONAL WRITING

Read the apartment ad in Exercise 6 on page 119. Does the apartment sound good to you? Why or why not? What features are important to you in a home? Write a paragraph. Use some of the adjectives and adverbs from the box.

beautiful	good	nice	residential
convenient	inexpensive	old	safe
extremely	large	quiet	terribly
friendly	modern	really	very

EXAMPLE: The apartment in the ad sounds very good. I like the fact that it is located in a residential neighborhood. It's really important to me to live in a quiet building . . .

_____

_____

_____

_____

_____

_____

_____

_____

_____

_____

_____

EXERCISE 1 SPELLING: REGULAR AND IRREGULAR COMPARATIVES

Write the comparative forms of the adjectives.

Adjective	Comparative
1. amazing	*more amazing*
2. bad	
3. big	
4. careful	
5. cheap	
6. comfortable	
7. crowded	
8. delicious	
9. early	
10. expensive	
11. far	
12. fresh	
13. good	
14. hot	
15. noisy	
16. relaxed	
17. terrible	
18. traditional	
19. varied	
20. wet	

EXERCISE 2 COMPARISONS WITH AS . . . AS

Look at the information comparing two pizza restaurants. Complete the sentences with
just as . . . as or *not as . . . as* and the correct form of the words in parentheses.

	PIZZA PALACE	JOE'S PIZZERIA
Year opened	2000	2000
Number of tables	40	20
Pizza size	12 inches	12 inches
Price of a cheese pizza	$10.00	$10.00
Choice of pizza toppings	15	7
Average waiting time for a table	10 minutes	5 minutes
Hours	noon–11:00 p.m. (7 days a week)	noon–8:00 p.m. (closed Mondays)
Atmosphere	★★	★
Service	★★	★★
Cleanliness	★★	★★
Food	★★	★★★

1. The Pizza Palace is _____*just as old as*_____ Joe's Pizzeria.
   (old)

2. Joe's Pizzeria is _____ the Pizza Palace.
   (large)

3. A pizza from Joe's Pizzeria is _____ the one from the Pizza Palace.
   (big)

4. The pizza at the Pizza Palace is _____ the pizza at Joe's Pizzeria.
   (expensive)

5. The choice of toppings at Joe's Pizzeria is _____ the choice at the
   (varied)

   Pizza Palace.

6. The waiting time at Joe's Pizzeria is _____ it is at the Pizza Palace.
   (long)

7. The hours at Joe's Pizzeria are _____ the hours at the Pizza Palace.
   (convenient)

8. Closing hour at Joe's Pizzeria is _____ it is at the Pizza Palace.
   (late)

9. The atmosphere at Joe's Pizzeria is _____ it is at the Pizza Palace.
   (nice)

10. The service at Joe's Pizzeria is _____ the service at the Pizza Palace.
    (good)

11. Joe's Pizzeria is _____ the Pizza Palace.
    (clean)

12. The pizza at the Pizza Palace is _____ it is at Joe's Pizzeria.
    (good)

EXERCISE 3 COMPARATIVES WITH *THAN*

These conversations took place at the Pizza Palace. Complete the conversations with the correct form of the adjectives in parentheses. Use *than* when necessary.

1. **A:** Wow, this place has gotten really popular!

   B: I know. It's even ___*more popular than*___ Joe's Pizzeria.
   (popular)

2. **A:** I can't believe how long the line is!

   B: Maybe we should come for an _____ dinner next time.
   (early)

3. **A:** I prefer that table over there.

   B: Me, too. It looks _____.
   (comfortable)

4. **A:** Let's order pizza number 7—with spinach, mushrooms, and tomatoes.

   B: OK. That sounds _____ the one with pepperoni and extra cheese.
   (healthy)

5. **A:** Mmm. This pizza is delicious. It's _____ the traditional kind.
   (interesting)

   B: It *is* good, but I still think the pizza at Joe's is even _____ the pizza
   (good)

   here. And Joe's ingredients always seem somewhat _____ to me.
   (fresh)

   Anyhow, that's just my opinion.

6. **A:** Hey, is that Brian over there at that table?

   B: No. Brian is much _____ that guy.
   (tall)

7. **A:** It sure is noisy in here. It's probably _____ on weekends.
   (bad)

   B: But it's a lot _____ at Joe's! And the atmosphere is
   (quiet)

   _____, too.
   (relaxed)

8. **A:** It's already 8:00.

   B: Oh! I thought it was _____ that.
   (late)

9. **A:** Do you ever make pizza yourself?

   B: No. I buy it frozen. It's _____ just to pop it in the microwave.
   (fast)

10. **A:** I really should buy a microwave oven.

    B: You really should. It will make your life _____.
    (easy)

EXERCISE 4 COMPARATIVES WITH *THAN*

Look at the chart comparing two microwave ovens. Complete the sentences with the appropriate comparative form of the adjectives in parentheses and *than*. Also, fill in the blanks with the brand—X or Y.

	●	◐	○
	Better ←————→ Worse		

Brand	Price	Size (cubic ft.)	Weight (lbs.)	Defrosting	Heating	Speed	Noise
X	$ 79	0.7	31	●	○	◐	○
Y	$ 65	0.9	36	◐	●	●	◐

1. Brand __X__ is ___more expensive than___ Brand __Y__.
   (expensive)

2. Brand ____ is _____ Brand ____.
   (cheap)

3. Brand ____ is _____ Brand ____.
   (large)

4. Brand ____ is _____ Brand ____.
   (small)

5. Brand ____ is _____ Brand ____.
   (heavy)

6. Brand ____ is _____ Brand ____.
   (light)

7. For defrosting food, Brand ____ is _____ Brand ____.
   (efficient)

8. For heating food, Brand ____ is _____ Brand ____.
   (effective)

9. Brand ____ is _____ Brand ____.
   (fast)

10. Brand ____ is _____ Brand ____.
    (slow)

11. Brand ____ is _____ Brand ____.
    (noisy)

12. Brand ____ is _____ Brand ____.
    (quiet)

13. In general, Brand ____ seems _____ Brand ____.
    (good)

14. In general, Brand ____ seems _____ Brand ____.
    (bad)

EXERCISE 5 COMPARATIVES TO EXPRESS INCREASE OR DECREASE

Look at the chart. It shows some food trends (increases and decreases). Complete the statements about the trends. Use the comparative forms of the adjectives from the box to show an increase or a decrease, or a cause and effect. Use both *more* and *less*.

| big | cheap | ~~expensive~~ | good | healthy | heavy | popular | varied |

	1995	2005	2015
1. cost of a slice of pizza	$	$$	$$$
2. cost of a microwave oven	$$$	$$	$
3. quality of frozen pizza	+	++	+++
4. restaurant portion size	+	++	+++
5. choice of pizza toppings	+	++	+++
6. popularity of fast food	+	++	+++
7. health quality of fast food	+++	++	+
8. weight of fast-food customers	+	++	+++

1. A slice of pizza is getting *more and more expensive* _____.

2. A microwave oven is getting _____.

3. The quality of frozen pizza is getting _____.

4. The size of portions in restaurants is getting _____.

5. The choice of pizza toppings is getting _____.

6. Fast food is becoming _____.

7. It's also becoming _____.

8. Fast-food customers are becoming _____.

EXERCISE 6 CAUSE AND EFFECT WITH TWO COMPARATIVES

Read the information. Write a similar sentence using two comparatives.

1. When the pizza is salty, I get thirsty.

The saltier the pizza, the thirstier I get. _____

2. When the ingredients are fresh, the food is good.

_____

(continued on next page)

3. When the restaurant is popular, the lines are long.

_____

4. When the meal is enjoyable, the customers are satisfied.

_____

5. When the selection is big, the customers are happy.

_____

6. When it's late in the day, the servers get tired.

_____

7. When the restaurant is crowded, the service is slow.

_____

8. When the service is good, the tip is high.

_____

EXERCISE 7 EDITING

Read the journal entry. There are eight mistakes in the use of comparisons. The first one is already corrected. Find and correct seven more.

I just got home from the Pizza Palace. Wow! The pizza there just keeps getting ~~good~~ better
and better. And, of course, the better the food, the more long the lines, and the

crowdeder the restaurant! But I don't really mind. It's totally worth it. Tonight, Ana

and I shared a pizza with spinach, mushrooms, and fresher tomatoes. It was much

more interesting as a traditional pizza with just tomato sauce and cheese. It's also

healthier than. And the ingredients were as fresh than you can find anywhere in the

city. (Although I usually think the pizza at Joe's Pizzeria is fresher.) It was so large that

we couldn't finish it, so I brought the rest home. Actually, I'm getting hungry again

just thinking about it. I think I'll pop a slice into the microwave and warm it up. It will

probably taste almost as better as it tasted at the Pizza Palace!

EXERCISE 8 PERSONAL WRITING

What is your opinion? Write a paragraph about two meals you have recently eaten.
Compare the experiences. Where did you eat? What did you have? How did you like it?
Use the comparative form of some of the adjectives from the box.

big	fast	healthy	noisy
expensive	good	interesting	relaxing

EXAMPLE: Recently, I ate in the school cafeteria. It was better than I expected. I had a chicken
sandwich and a cup of tomato soup. The food was a lot cheaper than the food at the
corner restaurant, and many of the choices were much . . .

_____

_____

_____

_____

_____

_____

_____

_____

_____

_____

_____

Adjectives: Superlatives

EXERCISE 1 SPELLING: REGULAR AND IRREGULAR SUPERLATIVES

Write the superlative form of the adjectives.

Adjective	Superlative
1. amazing	*the most amazing*
2. bad	
3. big	
4. cute	
5. dynamic	
6. expensive	
7. far	
8. funny	
9. good	
10. happy	
11. hot	
12. important	
13. intelligent	
14. interesting	
15. low	
16. nice	
17. noisy	
18. practical	
19. warm	
20. wonderful	

EXERCISE 2 THE SUPERLATIVE

Look at the information comparing the subway systems in three cities. Complete the sentences with the superlative form of the adjectives in parentheses. Also, write the name of the correct city.

THREE NORTH AMERICAN SUBWAY SYSTEMS			
	Toronto	New York City	Mexico City
First opened	1954	1904	1969
Length (miles)	42.4[1]	233.5	140.7
Number of riders (per year)	400 million	1.8 billion	1.7 billion
Cost of a single ride*	$2.32	$2.75	$0.27

[1](and an additional 17.1 miles under construction)
*in U.S. dollars

1. _____New York City_____ has _____the oldest_____ subway system.
   (old)

2. _____ has _____ subway system.
   (new)

3. _____'s system is _____.
   (long)

4. _____'s system is _____.
   (short)

5. _____ system is in _____.
   (busy)

6. _____ has _____ number of riders.
   (low)

7. The subway in _____ is _____ to use.
   (expensive)

8. You can buy _____ single ticket in _____.
   (cheap)

EXERCISE 3 SUPERLATIVE ADJECTIVES

Read the comments posted on an online subway message board. Complete the sentences with the superlative form of the correct adjectives from the boxes. Use *the -est* or *the most / the least*.

Track Talk

beautiful	big	easy	new	~~old~~

I just got back from London. Completed in 1863, the Tube (that's what they call their

subway) is _____the oldest_____ in the world, but it works just fine!
  1.

Sheppard Subway is _____ metro line in Toronto. It was
  2.

completed in 2002. I just rode it. Very nice!

IMHO (In my humble[1] opinion), the Moscow subway stations are without question

_____ in the world. They have some really nice features.
  3.

Statues, chandeliers, and artwork on the walls make them look more like museums

than stations! It's also one of _____ systems to use. There are
  4.

plenty of maps and signs in the stations so you don't get lost. As you can see, I'm one

of _____ fans of this great public transportation system!
  5.

comfortable	convenient	cool	dangerous	fast	hot	interesting

I just got back from a week's vacation in New York City. We had a great time and

rode the subway a lot. I have to say the subway seats are _____
  6.

I've ever experienced! They are so hard. I heard they used to be made of straw.[2] In any

case, it's _____ way to get around town—no traffic to slow you
  7.

down. It's summer, and all the trains are air-conditioned. Get ready for one of

_____

[1] *humble:* not considering your ideas as important or as good as other people's
[2] *straw:* dried stems of wheat or similar plants

_____ rides you've ever been on. In contrast, the stations are
8.

among _____ I've ever been in. I'm sure the temperature was
9.

over 100 degrees Fahrenheit. That said, New York has one of _____
10.

systems in the world. It's open 24 hours a day, 7 days a week, and you can go all over

the place—even to the beach! And I think it's _____ form of
11.

transportation to take. You see all kinds of people. It's a very multicultural experience.

Really fascinating. And this may really surprise you, but some people say it's one of

_____ subway systems because there are so many people on it.
12.

You're almost never alone—even late at night. I guess there's safety in numbers!

| crowded | dangerous | efficient | expensive | historic | quiet |

The subway in Athens is probably _____ in the world. When
13.

they were building the system, they found the remains of ancient roads, shops, and

baths. They've made these part of the system.

Tokyo has _____ subway in the world. At rush hour, there are
14.

so many people that special workers have to help push them onto the trains.

Driving in Paris? Don't even think about it! _____ way of
15.

getting around is the Metro. As in all big cities, you need to be careful and watch your

personal belongings. Rush hour is definitely _____ time to ride
16.

the subway because there can be pickpockets "working" the trains.

I love the subway system in Mexico City. First of all, at just 5 pesos (about 27 cents), it's

_____ ride in town (actually, in the whole world!). And because
17.

the train has rubber wheels, it's one of _____ rides, too.
18.

EXERCISE 4 EDITING

Read the tourist's postcard. There are seven mistakes in the use of the superlative. The first mistake is already corrected. Find and correct six more.

Hola!

   Greetings from Mexico City! With its mixture of the old
and the new, this is one of the ~~interestingest~~ <ins>most interesting</ins> cities I've
ever visited. The people are among the friendlier in the world, and they
have been very patient with my attempts to speak their language.
Spanish is definitely one of a most beautiful languages, and I really
want to take lessons when I get home.

   This has been the most hot summer in years, and I'm looking
forward to going to the beach next week. The air pollution is also the
baddest I've experienced, so I'll be glad to be out of the city.

   By the way, we definitely did not need to rent a car. The most fast
and convenientest way to get around is by subway.

See you soon.

L.

EXERCISE 5 PERSONAL WRITING

Write a paragraph about your city or country. What are some of the best things about it?
The worst? Use the superlative form of some of the adjectives from the box.

affordable	clean	easy	interesting
bad	convenient	friendly	nice
beautiful	difficult	good	safe

EXAMPLE: One of the best things about living here is the people. They are among the friendliest
and most interesting people I've ever met...

_____

_____

_____

_____

_____

_____

_____

_____

_____

_____

_____

Adverbs: *As ... as*, Comparatives, Superlatives

EXERCISE 1 SPELLING: REGULAR AND IRREGULAR COMPARATIVE AND SUPERLATIVE FORMS OF ADVERBS

Write the comparative and superlative forms of the adverbs.

Adverb	Comparative	Superlative
1. aggressively	*more aggressively*	*the most aggressively*
2. badly		
3. beautifully		
4. carefully		
5. consistently		
6. dangerously		
7. early		
8. effectively		
9. far		
10. fast		
11. frequently		
12. hard		
13. intensely		
14. little		
15. long		
16. much		
17. quickly		
18. slowly		
19. soon		
20. well		

EXERCISE 2 COMPARISONS OF ADVERBS WITH *AS . . . AS*

Look at the track-and-field records for five athletes. Complete the statements with the words in parentheses and *(not) as . . . as.*

	100-METER RUN	HIGH JUMP	DISCUS THROW
Athlete A	12.0 sec.	1.8 m	37 m
Athlete B	14.0 sec.	1.6 m	39 m
Athlete C	13.5 sec.	1.9 m	38 m
Athlete D	14.0 sec.	1.9 m	39 m
Athlete E	15.0 sec.	2.0 m	40 m

1. Athlete B ___*didn't run as fast as*___ Athlete A.
   (run / fast)

2. Athlete B _____ Athlete D.
   (run / fast)

3. Athlete C _____ Athlete D.
   (jump / high)

4. Athlete A _____ Athlete E.
   (jump / high)

5. Athlete C _____ Athlete E.
   (throw the discus / far)

6. Athlete D _____ Athlete B.
   (throw the discus / far)

7. In general, Athlete B _____ Athlete E.
   (do / good)

8. In general, Athlete A _____ Athlete C.
   (compete / successful)

EXERCISE 3 THE COMPARATIVE FORM OF ADVERBS

Basketball players from two teams are talking about their last game. Complete their comments. Use the correct form of the words in parentheses. Use *than* when necessary.

GEORGE: The other team played well, but we played much ___*better*___.
                                                        1. (good)

That's why we won.

🏀 🏀 🏀 🏀

JAMIL: We played _____ our opponents. We really deserved to win,
                      2. (hard)

and we did.

🏀 🏀 🏀 🏀

ALEX: It wasn't a great game for me. I moved _____ usual because of my
                                              3. (slow)

bad ankle. In a few weeks, I should be able to run _____. I hope
                                                    4. (fast)

that'll help the team.

(continued on next page)

RICK: Our shooting was off today. We missed too many baskets. We need to shoot a lot

_____ if we want to win.
　　5. (consistent)

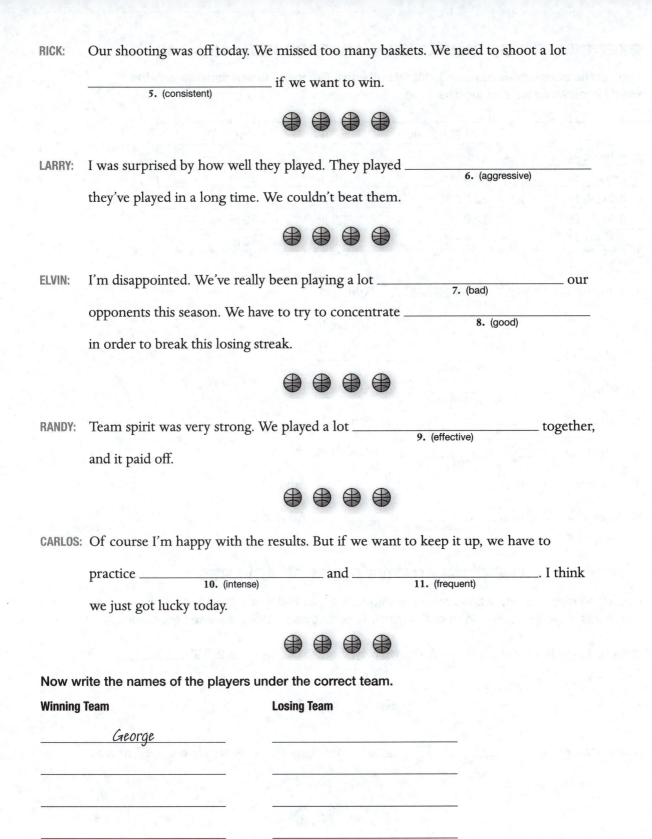

LARRY: I was surprised by how well they played. They played _____
　　　　　　　　　　　　　　　　　　　　　　　　　　　　　6. (aggressive)

they've played in a long time. We couldn't beat them.

ELVIN: I'm disappointed. We've really been playing a lot _____ our
　　　　　　　　　　　　　　　　　　　　　　　　　　　7. (bad)

opponents this season. We have to try to concentrate _____
　　　　　　　　　　　　　　　　　　　　　　　　　　　　　8. (good)

in order to break this losing streak.

RANDY: Team spirit was very strong. We played a lot _____ together,
　　　　　　　　　　　　　　　　　　　　　　　　　　9. (effective)

and it paid off.

CARLOS: Of course I'm happy with the results. But if we want to keep it up, we have to

practice _____ and _____. I think
　　　　　　10. (intense)　　　　　　　　　　　11. (frequent)

we just got lucky today.

Now write the names of the players under the correct team.

Winning Team　　　　　　　　　**Losing Team**

_____George_____　　_____

_____　　_____

_____　　_____

_____　　_____

EXERCISE 4 THE COMPARATIVE AND SUPERLATIVE OF ADVERBS

Look at the chart in Exercise 2 on page 135. Complete the statements with the correct form of the words in parentheses. Use *than* when necessary. Then complete the statements with the letter of the correct athlete—*A, B, C, D,* or *E.*

1. Athlete B ran _____*faster than*_____ Athlete __E__, but Athlete __A__ ran
   (fast)
   _____*the fastest*_____ of all.
   (fast)

2. Athlete _____ ran _____. He ran _____ all the
   (slow)   (slow)
   other competitors.

3. Athlete A jumped _____ Athlete _____.
   (high)

4. Athlete _____ jumped _____ of all five athletes.
   (high)

5. Athletes B and D didn't throw the discus _____ Athlete _____.
   (far)

6. Athlete _____ threw the discus _____.
   (far)

7. Athlete _____ won in two categories. He performed _____.
   (good)

8. At 15 seconds, Athlete _____ scored _____ in the run, but he did
   (bad)
   _____ the other athletes in the rest of the events.
   (good)

EXERCISE 5 THE COMPARATIVE OF ADVERBS TO EXPRESS CHANGE

Read about some athletes. Write a summary statement about each situation. Use the correct form of the words from the box.

accurate	dangerous	~~fast~~	graceful	long
bad	far	frequent	high	slow

1. Last month, Lisa ran a mile in 12 minutes. This month, she's running a mile in eight minutes.

   SUMMARY: *She's running faster and faster.* _____

2. Last month, she ran three times a week. This month, she's running every day.

   SUMMARY: _____

3. Last month, Josh threw the ball 10 yards. This month, he's throwing it 13 yards.

   SUMMARY: _____

4. Last month, when Jennifer shot baskets, she got only five balls in. Now, when she shoots baskets, she gets at least eight balls in.

   SUMMARY: _____

(continued on next page)

5. Six months ago, Mike jumped four and a half feet. Now, he's jumping almost six feet.

SUMMARY: _____

6. Matt used to run an eight-minute mile. These days, he runs a 10-minute mile.

SUMMARY: _____

7. The ice-dancing team of Sonia and Boris used to score about 30 points for their elegant dancing.

These days, they are scoring more than 40 points.

SUMMARY: _____

8. The basketball team used to practice two hours a day. Now, they practice three.

SUMMARY: _____

9. Jason drives a race car. Last year, he had two accidents. This year, he's had five.

SUMMARY: _____

10. Last year, the team felt good about their game. Now, they feel terrible.

SUMMARY: _____

EXERCISE 6 EDITING

Read Luisa's online exercise journal. There are seven mistakes in the use of adverbs. The first mistake is already corrected. Find and correct six more.

Tuesday, June 11

                                                                           than

I just completed my run. I'm running much longer ~~that~~ before.

Wednesday, June 12

Today I ran for 30 minutes without getting out of breath. I'm glad I decided to run more slow.

The more slowly I run, the farthest I can go. I'm really seeing progress.

Thursday, June 13

Because I'm enjoying it, I run more and more frequent. And the more often I do it, the longer

and farther I can go. I really believe that running helps me feel better more quick than other

forms of exercise. I'm even sleeping better than before!

Friday, June 14

I'm thinking about running in the next marathon. I may not run as fast than younger runners, but

I think I can run long and farther. We'll see!

EXERCISE 7 PERSONAL WRITING

Write a paragraph about your English skills. How are you speaking? Are you understanding what you hear? How is your reading? Writing? Use the adverb forms of the words from the box (or your own ideas).

accurate	fluent	hard
easy	frequent	quick
fast	good	slow

EXAMPLE: I think my English skills are really improving. I'm speaking more fluently, and . . .

_____

_____

_____

_____

_____

_____

_____

_____

_____

_____

_____

Gerunds: Subject and Object

EXERCISE 1 GERUNDS AS SUBJECT AND AS OBJECT

Complete the article from a health magazine. Use the gerund form of the verbs in parentheses.

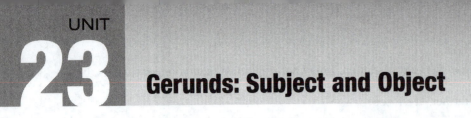

KICK UP YOUR HEELS!

In recent years, _____dancing_____ has become a very popular
                    1. (dance)

way to stay in shape. In addition to its health benefits, it also has social

advantages. "I really enjoy _____ out and
                            2. (go)

_____ new people," says Diana Romero, a 28-year-old web developer.
3. (meet)

"_____ all day at a computer isn't healthy. After work, I need to move." And
  4. (sit)

Diana isn't alone on the dance floor. Many other people who dislike _____,
                                                                    5. (run)

_____ weights, or _____ sit-ups are swaying to the beat of the
      6. (lift)   **7. (do)**

swing, salsa, and rumba.

So, if you are looking for an enjoyable way to build muscles and friendships, consider

_____ a spin on one of the many studio dance floors that are opening up in
  8. (take)

cities across the country. "_____ can be fun," says Sandra Carrone, owner of
                          9. (exercise)

Studio Two-Step. So, quit _____ time, grab a partner, and kick up your heels!
                          10. (waste)

EXERCISE 2 GERUNDS AS SUBJECT AND AS OBJECT

Look at the results of this questionnaire on four students' likes and dislikes. Then complete the sentences below with appropriate gerunds.

	KATIE	RYAN	LUKE	ANA
Dance	+	+	+	+
Walk	+	+	✓	✓
Do sit-ups	−	−	−	−
Play tennis	+	−	+	✓
Run	−	+	+	+
Lift weights	−	✓	−	+
Swim	✓	+	−	✓
Ride a bike	+	+	✓	+

Key: + enjoy
       ✓ don't mind
       − dislike

1. Ryan is the only one who dislikes _____ *playing tennis* _____.

2. _____ is the group's favorite activity.

3. Half the people dislike _____.

4. Half the people enjoy _____ and _____.

5. Katie and Ana don't mind _____.

6. Ana is the only one who enjoys _____.

7. Luke doesn't mind _____ or _____.

8. _____ is the most disliked activity.

9. Luke is the only one who dislikes _____.

10. He also doesn't like _____ or _____.

11. Katie is the only one who doesn't like _____.

12. Katie and Luke really like _____, but Ryan dislikes it.

13. _____ is the group's second favorite activity.

14. Ryan doesn't mind _____.

EXERCISE 3 GERUNDS AFTER CERTAIN VERBS

Sandra Carrone is having a dance party at her studio. Complete the summary sentences with the appropriate verbs from the box and the gerund form of the verbs in parentheses.

admit	consider	dislike	keep	permit	regret
ban	deny	enjoy	mind	~~quit~~	suggest

1. **LUKE:** Would you like a cup of coffee?

   KATIE: No, thanks. I haven't had coffee in five years.

   SUMMARY: Katie _____*quit drinking*_____ coffee five years ago.
   (drink)

2. **OSCAR:** Oh, they're playing a tango. Would you like to dance?

   RIKA: No, thanks. It's not my favorite dance.

   SUMMARY: Rika _____ the tango.
   (do)

3. **ANA:** Do you often come to these dance parties?

   MARIA: Yes. It's a good opportunity to dance with a lot of different partners.

   SUMMARY: Maria _____ with different partners.
   (dance)

4. **LAURA:** I don't know how to do the cha-cha. Could you show me?

   BILL: OK. Just follow me.

   SUMMARY: Bill doesn't _____ Laura the cha-cha.
   (teach)

5. **KATIE:** This is a difficult dance. How did you learn it?

   LUKE: I practiced it over and over again.

   SUMMARY: Luke _____ the dance.
   (practice)

6. **VERA:** Ow. You stepped on my toe!

   LUIS: No, I didn't!

   SUMMARY: Luis _____ on Vera's toe.
   (step)

7. **BILL:** Are you going to take any more classes?

   LAURA: I'm not sure. I haven't decided yet. Maybe.

   SUMMARY: Laura is _____ more dance classes.
   (take)

8. **KATIE:** I really love dancing.

   LUKE: Me, too. I'm sorry I didn't start years ago. It's a lot of fun.

   SUMMARY: Luke _____ dance lessons sooner.
   (not begin)

9. BILL: Why don't we go out for coffee after class next week?

LAURA: OK. I'd like that.

SUMMARY: Bill _____ out after class.
(go)

10. LUKE: You look tired.

LAURA: I *am* tired. I think this will be the last dance for me.

SUMMARY: Laura _____ tired.
(feel)

11. DAN: Would you like a cigarette?

INA: I don't smoke. Besides, it isn't permitted here.

SUMMARY: The studio _____.
(smoke)

12. DAN: You can't smoke in the studio?

INA: No. But you can smoke outside.

SUMMARY: The studio _____ outside.
(smoke)

EXERCISE 4 GERUNDS AFTER PREPOSITIONS

Complete the conversations with the correct preposition and the gerund form of the verbs in parentheses.

1. KYLE: Where were you? It's 7:30!

JOHN: I know. I apologize _____*for being*_____ late.
(be)

2. EMMA: Are you excited about your vacation?

JUSTIN: Oh, yes. I'm really looking forward _____ a break. I need one.
(have)

3. AUSTIN: I'm trying to stop smoking, but it's so hard.

NOAH: Don't give up. I'm sure you'll succeed _____.
(quit)

4. RYAN: What's wrong? You look upset.

SASHA: I have a test tomorrow, and I'm worried _____ it.
(pass)

5. CHENG: Where's José?

COLE: He's still at work. He insisted _____ late and
(stay)

_____ his report.
(finish)

(continued on next page)

6. KEVIN: I'm tired _____ home every night. Let's go out.
(stay)

    AMBER: Good idea. I'm in favor _____ out more.
(get)

7. KAYLA: I hear the school cafeteria is going to get a salad bar.

    MEGAN: That's great! I believe _____ healthy choices for lunch. It's really
(have)

    important.

8. JOHN: Do you approve _____ smoking outside the school building?
(permit)

    SIMON: Actually, I don't. I'm opposed _____ in public areas. They should
(smoke)

    prohibit it.

EXERCISE 5 EDITING

Read the online survey about smoking. There are seven mistakes in the use of gerunds.
The first one is already corrected. Find and correct six more.

Smoking Survey

Click on the statements you agree with.

               banning
- I'm in favor of ~~ban~~ smoking in all public places.

- I think to smoke should be illegal in parks and at beaches.

- I approve to having free programs that help people quit to smoke.

- To advertise cigarettes in newspapers and magazines is alright.

- Smoking cigarettes are a private decision, and the government should not

  make laws against it.

- If people enjoy to light up a cigarette, that is their right.

EXERCISE 6 PERSONAL WRITING

Look at the chart in Exercise 2 on page 141. How do you feel about the eight activities in the chart? Write a paragraph. Use some of the phrases from the box.

I can get tired of . . .	I really dislike . . .
I can't get excited about . . .	I sometimes look forward to . . .
I don't enjoy . . .	I would like to start . . .
I don't mind . . .	I'm not opposed to . . .
I enjoy . . .	I've never considered . . .

EXAMPLE: I know exercise is important. I try to do some every day, but there are some things I like better than others. Dancing is my favorite activity. I enjoy . . .

_____

_____

_____

_____

_____

_____

_____

_____

_____

_____

_____

_____

EXERCISE 1 INFINITIVES AFTER CERTAIN VERBS

Read the exchange of letters in an advice column. Complete the letters with the correct form of the verbs in parentheses. Use the simple present, simple past, or future for the first verb.

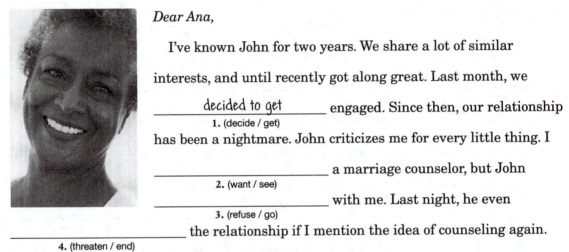

Dear Ana,

I've known John for two years. We share a lot of similar interests, and until recently got along great. Last month, we _____**decided to get**_____ engaged. Since then, our relationship
1. (decide / get)
has been a nightmare. John criticizes me for every little thing. I

_____ a marriage counselor, but John
2. (want / see)

_____ with me. Last night, he even
3. (refuse / go)

_____ the relationship if I mention the idea of counseling again.
4. (threaten / end)
I don't understand what's going on. I still love John, but I _____
5. (hesitate / take)
the next step. Can we solve our problems? What should I do?

ONE FOOT OUT THE DOOR

Dear One Foot Out the Door,

I've heard your story many times before. You're right to be concerned. Obviously, John

_____ afraid of getting married. As soon as you got engaged, he
6. (seem / be)

_____ distance by criticizing you. I agree that counseling is a good
7. (attempt / create)
idea if the two of you really _____ together. Maybe each of you
8. (intend / stay)

_____ to a counselor separately before going to one together. It's
9. (need / speak)
possible that John _____ alone to discuss some of his fears.
10. (agree / go)

ANA

EXERCISE 2 VERB + INFINITIVE OR VERB + OBJECT + INFINITIVE

Read the conversations between men and women in relationships. Complete the two summary statements for each conversation.

1. SHE: We need to focus on our relationship. I *really* think we should see a therapist.

   HE: Well, I'm not going to.

   SUMMARY: She urged *him to see a therapist.*

   He refused *to see a therapist.*

2. HE: Could you please do the dishes tonight?

   SHE: Sorry. I don't have time. Could you please do them?

   SUMMARY: He didn't want _____

   She wanted _____

3. HE: Don't forget to buy some milk.

   SHE: OK. I'll get some on the way home.

   SUMMARY: He reminded _____

   She agreed _____

4. SHE: Will you do me a favor? Could you drive me to my aunt's?

   HE: OK.

   SUMMARY: She asked _____

   He agreed _____

5. SHE: Would you like to have dinner at my place Friday night?

   HE: Um . . . I'm not sure. Um . . . I guess so.

   SUMMARY: She invited _____

   He hesitated _____

6. SHE: Will you give me your answer tomorrow?

   HE: Yes, I will. That's a promise.

   SUMMARY: She wants _____

   He promised _____

(continued on next page)

7. SHE: Would you like me to cut your hair? It's really long.

     HE: Oh, OK.

     SUMMARY: She offered _____

     He is going to allow _____

8. SHE: It's 8:00. I thought you said you'd be home at 7:00.

     HE: No. I always get home at 8:00.

     SUMMARY: She expected _____

     He expected _____

9. HE: Why didn't you call me before you left the office?

     SHE: I was going to, but I forgot.

     SUMMARY: He wanted _____

     She intended _____

10. SHE: Let's see a movie Friday night.

     HE: OK, but could you pick one?

     SUMMARY: She would like _____

     He would like _____

11. HE: I plan on asking my boss for a raise.

     SHE: Great idea. I think you definitely should do it.

     SUMMARY: He intends _____

     She's encouraging _____

12. SHE: I'd like to get some more stamps.

     HE: Oh, I'll stop at the post office on the way home.

     SUMMARY: She wants _____

     He volunteered _____

EXERCISE 3 EDITING

Read the journal entry. There are ten mistakes in the use of infinitives. The first mistake is already corrected. Find and correct nine more.

Ana answered my letter. I didn't expect ~~hearing~~ (to hear) back from her so soon! She agrees that seeing a counselor is a good idea for John and me, but she advised we to go to counseling separately at first. That idea never even occurred to me, but I think that it's a really excellent suggestion. I don't know if John will agree going, but I'm definitely going to ask him to think about it when I see him on Saturday. I attempted to introduce the topic last night, but he pretended to not hear me. (He's been doing that a lot lately. He seems to think if he ignores a question, I'll just forget about it!) I won't give up, though. I'm going to try to persuade he to go. I have no idea how to find a counselor, so if he agrees to go, I may ask Ana recommend someone in our area. Obviously, I want finding someone really good.

I still believe in us as a couple. Our relationship deserves to have a chance, and I'm prepared give it one. But I want John feels the same way. After all, it takes more than one person to make a relationship. I really need to know that he's 100 percent committed to the relationship. I can be patient, but I can't afford waiting forever.

EXERCISE 4 PERSONAL WRITING

What do you expect from your friends? Write one or two paragraphs. Use some of the phrases from the box or ideas of your own.

I count on them . . .	I prefer (them) . . .
I don't expect them . . .	I really need (them) . . .
I expect my friends . . .	I would like (them) . . .

EXAMPLE: Friends are really important to me. I expect my friends to always tell me the truth.
When I have a problem, I count on them . . .

_____

_____

_____

_____

_____

_____

_____

_____

_____

_____

_____

UNIT 25 More Uses of Infinitives

EXERCISE 1 INFINITIVES OF PURPOSE: AFFIRMATIVE STATEMENTS

Look at the chart. Nate has an old cell phone and a new smartphone. Make sentences with the words in parentheses.

NATE'S OLD AND NEW PHONES		
	OLD CELL PHONE	**NEW SMART PHONE**
make calls	●	●
take pictures	●	●
search online		●
send emails		●
connect to the Internet	●	●
create a "To Do" list		●
store addresses	●	●
play music		●
translate words		●

1. _Nate can use his cell phone or smartphone to make calls._
   (make calls)

2. _____
   (take pictures)

3. _____
   (search online)

4. _____
   (send emails)

5. _____
   (connect to the Internet)

6. _____
   (create a "To Do" list)

7. _____
   (store addresses)

8. _____
   (play music)

9. _____
   (translate words)

EXERCISE 2 INFINITIVES OF PURPOSE: AFFIRMATIVE AND NEGATIVE STATEMENTS

Combine these pairs of sentences. Use the infinitive of purpose.

1. Ed got a job at Edge Electronics. He needs to earn money for school.

   Ed got a job at Edge Electronics to earn money for school.

2. Ed never brings money to work. He doesn't want to buy a lot of stuff.

   Ed never brings money to work in order not to buy a lot of stuff.

3. He uses most of his salary. He has to pay his college tuition.

   _____

4. He really wants a smartwatch. He wants to read text messages while jogging.

   _____

5. He's going to wait for a sale. Then he won't pay the full price.

   _____

6. A lot of people came into the store today. They looked at the new multipurpose devices.

   _____

7. They like talking to Ed. They want to get information about the devices.

   _____

8. Someone bought a GPS. He doesn't want to get lost.

   _____

9. Another person bought a robot vacuum. She wants to do less housework.

   _____

10. She used her credit card. She didn't want to pay right away.

    _____

11. Ed showed her how to use the robot vacuum. It can clean a large room.

    _____

12. She'll use it in her apartment. She'll save time.

    _____

EXERCISE 3 INFINITIVES AFTER ADJECTIVES

Some people are talking at a mall. Complete the conversations with the verbs from the box and the infinitive of purpose.

| eat | find | have | ~~keep up~~ | leave | pay | take |

1. **A:** I need to go to Edge Electronics.

   B: How come?

   A: I've decided to get a new smartphone. It's important _____*to keep up*_____ with the latest technology!

2. **A:** I'd like to return this GPS.

   B: Do you have the receipt?

   A: No, I don't. I got it as a gift.

   B: Hmmm. I see that there's no price tag on it. I'm very sorry, but it really is necessary _____ the receipt in order to return it.

3. **A:** Why don't you use your credit card?

   B: I know it's convenient _____ with a credit card, but I prefer to use cash for small purchases. Call me old-fashioned!

4. **A:** I'm hungry. How's the food court here?

   B: It's actually very nice _____ there. The food is pretty good and there's a great view of the capitol building.

5. **A:** That was a good lunch. I'm ready _____ now. What about you?

   B: Sure. I'm done shopping. Let's go.

6. **A:** Well, here's the escalator.

   B: It's faster _____ the elevator. And it's right over there.

7. **A:** Do you want to see a movie?

   B: OK. But we don't have a movie schedule with us.

   A: No problem! I have my smartphone. It's easy _____ a movie with it. Let's see what's playing around here.

EXERCISE 4 INFINITIVES AFTER ADJECTIVES AND ADVERBS + *TOO* OR *ENOUGH*

Complete the conversations. Use the words in parentheses with the infinitive and *too* or *enough*.

1. A: Did you get a new smartphone at the mall?

   B: No. It was still ___too expensive for me to get___.
   (expensive / me / get)

2. A: Are you really that unhappy with the phone you have now?

   B: Not really. It's _____ almost everything I need to do. I just would
   (good / me / do)

   like it to have some more functions.

3. A: Do you want to go to a movie tonight?

   B: It's 10:00 already. It's _____.
   (late / go)

4. A: Maybe we can go tomorrow night.

   B: Sure, if we finish dinner _____ by 7:00.
   (fast / leave)

5. A: I have an idea. Why don't we combine a movie with a late-night dinner afterward?

   B: OK. That is, if I'm not _____ awake!
   (tired / stay)

6. A: Do you think I can call Alicia now?

   B: At 10:00? Sure. It's not _____.
   (late / call)

7. A: Do you have trouble understanding her on the phone?

   B: Who, Alicia? Not at all. She always speaks _____.
   (clearly / me / understand)

8. A: Could you please turn on the air conditioner?

   B: The air conditioner? It's not _____ the air conditioner!
   (hot / need)

9. A: You're not drinking your tea. What's wrong with it?

   B: Nothing. It's just still _____.
   (hot / me / drink)

10. A: How does Dan like his new phone?

    B: He likes it, and it's _____.
    (easy / him / program)

EXERCISE 5 EDITING

Read the text messages. There are eight mistakes in the use of the infinitive of purpose and infinitives after adjectives. The first mistake is already corrected. Find and correct seven more. Check spelling, too.

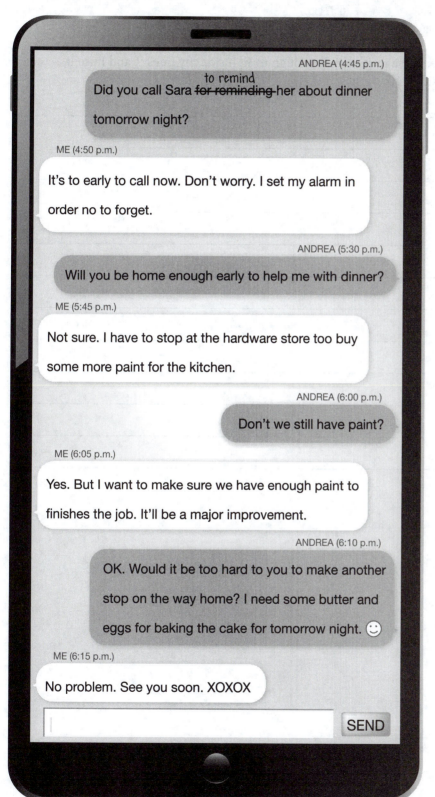

ANDREA (4:45 p.m.)
Did you call Sara ~~for reminding~~ *to remind* her about dinner tomorrow night?

ME (4:50 p.m.)
It's to early to call now. Don't worry. I set my alarm in order no to forget.

ANDREA (5:30 p.m.)
Will you be home enough early to help me with dinner?

ME (5:45 p.m.)
Not sure. I have to stop at the hardware store too buy some more paint for the kitchen.

ANDREA (6:00 p.m.)
Don't we still have paint?

ME (6:05 p.m.)
Yes. But I want to make sure we have enough paint to finishes the job. It'll be a major improvement.

ANDREA (6:10 p.m.)
OK. Would it be too hard to you to make another stop on the way home? I need some butter and eggs for baking the cake for tomorrow night. ☺

ME (6:15 p.m.)
No problem. See you soon. XOXOX

SEND

EXERCISE 6 PERSONAL WRITING

Imagine you just got a new smartphone. What do you use it for? How do you like it? Write
a paragraph. Use infinitives and some of the words from the box (or your own ideas).

| convenient | expensive | good | (not) too |
| easy | fun | (not) enough | small |

EXAMPLE: I just got a new phone. I love it. It's small enough to fit inside my pocket and I use it
to do many things besides talk. I use it . . .

_____

_____

_____

_____

_____

_____

_____

_____

_____

_____

EXERCISE 1 GERUND OR INFINITIVE

Read the notice about a support-group meeting for people who are afraid of flying. Complete the sentences with the correct form—gerund or infinitive—of the verbs in parentheses.

Stuck on the ground? Don't wait! Get help now!

Are you afraid of _____flying_____? Stop _____ in fear!
　　　　　　　　　　　　　1. (fly)　　　　　　　　　　　**2.** (live)

_____ is the safest form of transportation, but many people are too anxious
3. (fly)

_____ on a plane.
4. (get)

Do *you* avoid _____ because you're afraid to leave the ground? Would you
　　　　　　　　　5. (fly)

like _____ your fear?
　　　6. (get over)

Don't let your fear prevent you from _____ all the things that you want
　　　　　　　　　　　　　　　　　　　　7. (do)

_____. You deserve _____ a life free of fear. So, don't put it off.
8. (do)　　　　　　　　　　　**9.** (live)

Decide _____ something about your problem NOW. Come to our monthly
　　　　10. (do)

support-group meetings.

The next meeting is at 7:00 p.m., Tuesday, March 3 at the Community Center. We look

forward to _____ you there.
　　　　　11. (see)

And don't forget _____ our website at www.flyaway.com for some helpful
　　　　　　　　　　12. (visit)

tips on _____ yourself off the ground!
　　　13. (get)

EXERCISE 2 GERUND OR INFINITIVE

These conversations take place at a support-group meeting for people who are afraid of flying. Complete the summary statements about the people. Use the correct verbs or expressions from the box and the gerund or infinitive form of the verbs in parentheses.

afford	be tired of	enjoy	intend	~~quit~~	remember
agree	believe in	forget	offer	refuse	stop

1. **DYLAN:** Would you like a cup of coffee?

   SYLVIE: No, thanks. I gave up coffee. It makes me too anxious.

   SUMMARY: Sylvie _____ *quit drinking* _____ coffee.
   (drink)

2. **ANDREA:** Why did you start coming to these meetings?

   HANK: My fear of flying prevents me from doing too many things. It's very discouraging, and I finally want to do something about it.

   SUMMARY: Hank _____ afraid of flying.
   (be)

3. **JASON:** Have you ever been to one of these support-group meetings before?

   AMBER: Yes. I like meeting people with the same problem. You get a lot of useful tips.

   SUMMARY: Amber _____ people with the same problem.
   (meet)

4. **CARYN:** I think these meetings are really helpful. You can learn a lot when you talk to other people about your problems.

   PAULO: I agree.

   SUMMARY: Caryn _____ to other people about her problems.
   (talk)

5. **MARY:** Did you bring the travel guide?

   SARA: Oh, no. I left it at work.

   SUMMARY: Sara _____ the travel guide.
   (bring)

6. **AMANDA:** Did you tell Amy about tonight's meeting?

   JOSHUA: No, *you* told Amy about the meeting. I heard you do it.

   AMANDA: Really? Are you sure?

   SUMMARY: Amanda doesn't _____ Amy about the meeting.
   (tell)

7. **TYLER:** You're late. I was getting worried.

   EMILY: I'm sorry. On the way over here, I noticed that I was almost out of gas. So I went to fill up the tank.

   SUMMARY: Emily _____ gas.
   (get)

8. KATIE: I know your parents live in California. How do you get there?

MIKE: I take the train. It's a long trip, and I lose much too much time.

SUMMARY: Mike can't _____ the time.
(lose)

9. CAMILLE: I was afraid to come to the meeting tonight.

VILMA: Well, I just *won't* live in fear.

SUMMARY: Vilma _____ in fear.
(live)

10. ERIN: Have you made your flight reservations yet?

LUIS: Not yet. But I'm definitely going to do it.

SUMMARY: Luis _____ a reservation.
(make)

11. RACHEL: Do you think you could help us organize the next meeting?

JUSTIN: Sure. Just give me a task to do and I'll be glad to help.

RACHEL: We don't have a date yet, but I'll let you know.

SUMMARY: Justin _____ with the next meeting.
(help)

12. AXEL: Would you like a ride home?

JOANNA: Thanks. That would be great.

SUMMARY: Axel _____ Joanna home.
(drive)

EXERCISE 3 GERUND OR INFINITIVE

Rewrite the sentences. If the sentence uses the gerund, rewrite it with the infinitive. If the sentence uses the infinitive, rewrite it with the gerund.

1. It's important to talk about your problems.

   Talking about your problems is important.

2. Going to a support group is helpful.

   It's helpful to go to a support group.

3. Working together is useful.

   _____

4. It's smart to be careful.

   _____

(continued on next page)

5. It's not good to be anxious all the time.

_____

6. Flying isn't dangerous.

_____

7. Doing relaxation exercises is a good idea.

_____

8. Traveling is wonderful.

_____

EXERCISE 4 EDITING

Read Hank's post to a fear of flying forum. There are ten mistakes in the use of gerunds and infinitives. The first mistake is already corrected. Find and correct nine more.

● ● ●

Taking Off!

04-16-2016 04:59 a.m.

Things are looking up!

       to report
I want ~~reporting~~ on my progress. I'm very happy that I finally stopped to procrastinate and decided

doing something about my fear of flying. It was really getting in the way of my professional and social

life. To join this support group was one of the smartest decisions I've ever made.

Last week, I had a business meeting in Texas. Instead of drive all day to get there, I was able to getting

on a plane and be there in just a few hours. What a difference!

I remember to work on an important project once, and I actually had to drop out because it required a

lot of flying and I just couldn't do it. I was anxious all the time.

My fear was beginning to hurt my friendships, too. I was dating a woman I liked a lot and we were

supposed to go on a trip. I canceled at the last minute because it required to take a plane.

Now I'm looking forward to do a lot of traveling. I know fear of flying is a universal problem, but it

doesn't have to be mine! It's a big world out there, and I plan on enjoy it.

EXERCISE 5 PERSONAL WRITING

Write a paragraph about a situation that makes you feel anxious or afraid. What do you do when you feel that way? Use some of the phrases from the box with gerunds or infinitives.

I always try . . .	I keep . . .	I try to remember . . .
I avoid . . .	I never quit . . .	It's important . . .
I imagine myself . . .	I often pretend . . .	Sometimes I can't help . . .

EXAMPLE: I always get nervous before speaking in front of a group of people. As a result, I try to avoid getting into situations where I need to give a speech. When I can't avoid doing it, I . . .

_____

_____

_____

_____

_____

_____

_____

_____

_____

_____

_____

Reflexive and Reciprocal Pronouns

EXERCISE 1 REFLEXIVE PRONOUNS

Write the reflexive pronouns.

1. I _____ *myself* _____

2. my grandfather _____

3. the class _____

4. my aunt _____

5. you _____ or _____

6. people _____

7. life _____

8. we _____

EXERCISE 2 REFLEXIVE OR RECIPROCAL PRONOUNS

Circle the correct pronouns to complete the sentences.

1. Anna and Jim call (each other) / themselves every weekend.

2. They have worked with each other / themselves for five years.

3. Anna herself / himself has been with the same company for ten years.

4. It's a nice place. All of the employees consider one another / themselves lucky to be there.

5. They respect each other / each other's opinions.

6. The boss herself / itself is very nice.

7. She tells her employees, "Don't push themselves / yourselves too hard!"

8. Anna enjoys the job herself / itself, but she especially likes her co-workers.

9. My brother and I are considering applying for jobs there myself / ourselves.

10. We talk to each other / ourselves about it when we jog together.

EXERCISE 3 REFLEXIVE OR RECIPROCAL PRONOUNS

Complete the conversations. Use reflexive or reciprocal pronouns.

1. **A:** What was Marianna's reaction when she lost her job?

   B: At first she was shocked. Then she told _____*herself*_____ it's a chance to find a better job.

2. **A:** What do you do to maintain your relationship with the people you used to work with?

   B: We all live in different places now, but we call and email _____.

3. **A:** How does Miguel like his new job?

   B: Well, the job _____ isn't that interesting, but he really likes the people he works with.

4. **A:** So, you finally met Ina!

   B: Yes. I didn't realize that we had so much in common. We really enjoyed talking to _____.

5. **A:** Excuse me? I didn't hear what you just said. Could you please repeat it?

   B: Oh, it was nothing. I was just talking to _____! I do that from time to time. It's a habit.

6. **A:** Gina! Ricardo! Good to see you both. Come in and help _____ to some food and drinks.

   B: Thanks! We will.

   C: It looks great.

7. **A:** What happened to Frank's face?

   B: Oh, he cut _____ when he was shaving. It looks worse than it is.

8. **A:** You know, giving a party is a lot of work. Maybe we should think about this a little more.

   B: You're right. We need to ask _____ if we really have the time now.

9. **A:** How did you learn to play the guitar? Did you teach _____?

   B: No. A friend taught me.

10. **A:** Who are those two women over there?

    B: Oh, that's Olga and Marta. They just introduced _____ to me.

EXERCISE 4 VERBS WITH REFLEXIVE OR RECIPROCAL PRONOUNS

Gina had a party. Read each conversation and complete the summary. Use the correct form of the verbs in parentheses with an appropriate reflexive or reciprocal pronoun.

1. **JOYCE:** This party is a lot of fun.

   HANK: I've never danced with so many people in my life!

   SUMMARY: Joyce and Hank ___are enjoying themselves___.
   (enjoy)

2. **RON:** We were late because you forgot the address.

   MIA: It's not my fault. You never gave me the slip of paper!

   SUMMARY: Ron and Mia _____.
   (criticize)

3. **GINA:** I'm so glad you could come. There are food and drinks on that table over there.

   Why don't you take a plate and get some?

   CHEN: Thanks. I will. It all looks delicious.

   SUMMARY: Chen _____.
   (help)

4. **AMY:** OK, Amy. Now don't be shy. Go over and talk to that guy over there.

   TIM: Come on, Tim. You can do it. She's looking in your direction. Just go on over.

   SUMMARY: Amy and Tim _____.
   (talk)

5. **AMY:** Hi. I'm Amy.

   TIM: Hi. I'm Tim.

   SUMMARY: Amy and Tim _____.
   (introduce)

6. **AMY:** So, how do you know Gina?

   TIM: Oh, Gina and I were in the same class. What about you?

   SUMMARY: Amy and Tim _____.
   (talk)

7. **PAT:** Did you come with Doug?

   LAURA: No. Doug couldn't make it, but he let me use his car.

   SUMMARY: Laura _____.
   (drive)

8. **LIZ:** I'm sorry to hear about your job, Hank.

   HANK: It was my fault. I realize that I didn't take it seriously enough, but I've learned my

   lesson. It won't happen again.

   SUMMARY: Hank _____.
   (blame)

9. CARA: You know, I'm really glad we finally met.

    LIZ: Me too. I feel like we've known each other a long time.

    SUMMARY: Cara and Liz _____ company.
                                         (enjoy)

10. LIZ: It was a wonderful party. Thanks for inviting me.

    GINA: Thanks for coming. And thank you for the lovely flowers.

    SUMMARY: Liz and Gina _____.
                                   (thank)

EXERCISE 5 EDITING

Read Liz's journal entry. There are eleven mistakes in the use of reflexive and reciprocal pronouns. The first mistake is already corrected. Find and correct ten more.

April 25

                   myself

I really enjoyed ~~me~~ at Gina's party! Hank was there, and we talked to ourselves quite a bit. He's a little depressed about losing his job. The job himself wasn't that great, but the loss of income has really impacted his life. He's disappointed in himself. He thinks it's all his own fault, and he blames him for the whole thing.

Hank introduced myself to several of his friends. I spoke a lot to this one woman, Cara. We have a lot of things in common, and after just an hour, we felt like we had known each other's forever. Cara himself is a computer programmer, just like me.

At first, I was nervous about going to the party alone. I sometimes feel a little uncomfortable when I'm in a social situation by oneself. But this time was different. Before I went, I kept telling myself to relax. My roommate too kept telling myself, "Don't be so hard on you! Just have fun!" That's what I advised Hank to do, too.

Before we left the party, Hank and I promised us to keep in touch. I hope to see him again soon.

EXERCISE 6 PERSONAL WRITING

Imagine you went to a party last weekend. Who did you go with? What did you do there? Who did you meet? What did you talk about? Did you have a good time? Write a paragraph about the party. Use some of the verbs from the box with reflexive or reciprocal pronouns.

dance	enjoy	introduce	see
drive	help	know	talk

EXAMPLE: Last Friday night, I went to a party by myself. I didn't know anyone there, but I introduced myself to some people. I met a very interesting . . .

_____

_____

_____

_____

_____

_____

_____

_____

_____

_____

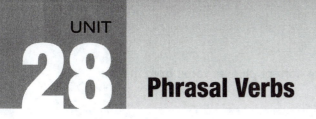

UNIT 28 Phrasal Verbs

EXERCISE 1 PARTICLES

Complete the phrasal verbs with particles from the box. You will use some particles more than once.

back	down	in	off	on	out	over	up

Phrasal Verb   **Definition**

1. call ___*off*___   cancel

2. call _____   return a phone call

3. come _____   enter

4. figure _____   solve

5. fill _____   complete

6. get _____   return

7. give _____   quit

8. go _____   continue

9. grow _____   become an adult

10. help _____   assist

11. look _____   be careful

12. point _____   indicate

13. take _____   get control of

14. take _____   remove

15. think _____   consider

16. turn _____   reject

17. turn _____   start a machine

18. work _____   exercise

EXERCISE 2 PHRASAL VERBS

Complete the handout for Professor Cho's class. Use the correct phrasal verbs from the box.

do over	help out	look up	~~pick up~~	talk over
hand in	look over	pick out	set up	write up

Science 101   Instructions for Writing the Term Paper   Prof. Cho

1. _____*Pick up*_____ a list of topics from the science department secretary.

2. _____ a topic that interests you. (If you are having problems choosing a topic, I'll be glad to _____ you _____.)

3. Go online. Use the Internet to _____ information on your chosen topic.

4. _____ an appointment with me to _____ your topic.

5. _____ your first draft.

6. _____ it _____ carefully. Check for accuracy of facts, spelling, and grammar errors.

7. _____ your report _____ if necessary.

8. _____ it _____ by May 28.

EXERCISE 3 PHRASAL VERBS AND OBJECT PRONOUNS

Complete the conversations between roommates. Use phrasal verbs and pronouns.

1. A: I haven't picked up the list of topics for our science paper yet.

   B: No problem. I'll _____*pick it up*_____ for you. I'm going to the science office later this afternoon.

2. A: Hey, guys. We've really got to clean up the kitchen. It's a mess.

   B: It's my turn to _____. I'll do it after dinner.

3. A: Did you remember to call your mom back?

   B: Oops! I'll _____ tonight.

4. A: Hey, can you turn down that music? I'm trying to concentrate.

   B: Sorry. I'll _____ right away.

5. A: It's after 9:00. Do you think we should wake John up?

   B: Don't _____. He said he wanted to sleep late.

6. **A:** Professor Cho turned down my science topic.

    B: Really? Why did she _____?

7. **A:** When do we have to hand in our reports?

    B: We have to _____ by Friday.

8. **A:** I wanted to drop off my report this afternoon, but I'm not going to have time.

    B: I can _____ for you. I have an appointment with Professor Cho

    at noon.

EXERCISE 4 WORD ORDER

Professor Cho made a list of things to do with her class. Unscramble the words to make sentences. In some cases, more than one answer is possible.

1. the homework problems / back / give

   Give back the homework problems. OR *Give the homework problems back.* _____

2. out / common mistakes / point

   _____

3. them / over / talk

   _____

4. a new problem / out / pick

   _____

5. it / out / work / with the class

   _____

6. up / the results / write

   _____

7. go / to the next unit / on

   _____

8. up / the final exam questions / make

   _____

9. them / out / hand

   _____

(continued on next page)

10. study groups / up / set

_____

11. out / them / help

_____

12. Friday's class / off / call

_____

EXERCISE 5 EDITING

Read the student's email. There are eleven mistakes in the use of phrasal verbs. The first mistake is already corrected. Find and correct ten more. A particle in the wrong place counts as one mistake.

● ● ●

Hi Katy!

How are things going? I'm already into the second month of the spring semester, and I've

got a lot of work to do. For science class, I have to write a term paper. The professor made ~~over~~ up

a list of possible topics. After looking over them, I think I've picked one out. I'm going to write

about chimpanzees and animal intelligence. I've already looked some information about them

online up. I found up some very interesting facts.

Did you know that their hands look very much like their feet,

and that they have fingernails and toenails? Their thumbs and big

toes are "opposable." This makes it easy for them to pick things

out with both their fingers and toes. Their arms are longer than

their legs. This helps out them, too, because they can reach fruit

growing on thin branches that would not otherwise support their weight. Adult males weigh

between 90 and 115 pounds (40 and 52 kilograms), and they are about 4 feet (1.2 meters) high

when they stand out.

Like humans, chimpanzees are very social. They travel in groups called "communities."

Mothers bring out their chimps, who stay with them until about the age of seven. Even after the

chimps grow up, there is still a lot of contact with other chimpanzees.

I could go on, but I need to stop writing now so I can clean out my room (it's a mess!) a little

before going to bed. It's late, and I have to get early up tomorrow morning for my 9:00 class.

Please let me know how you are. Or call me. I'm often out, but if you leave a message, I'll

call back you as soon as I can. It would be great to speak to you.

Best,

Tony

EXERCISE 6 PERSONAL WRITING

**How did you find out about this school? Write a paragraph about your experience
choosing the school and signing up for class. Use some of the phrasal verbs from the box.**

call up	find out	look up	talk over
figure out	help out	pick up	think over
fill out	look over	sign up	write down

EXAMPLE: I found out about this school from my neighbor. She's been a student here for
several years, and she helped me fill out the forms . . .

_____

_____

_____

_____

_____

_____

_____

_____

_____

_____

_____

Necessity: *Have (got) to, Must, Can't*

EXERCISE 1 AFFIRMATIVE AND NEGATIVE STATEMENTS WITH *MUST*

Read the driving rules. Complete the sentences with *must* or *must not* and the verbs from the box.

change	drive	~~have~~	leave	pass	stop	turn on
drink	forget	know	obey	sit	talk	wear

1. In almost all countries, you _____*must have*_____ a valid license in order to drive.

2. You _____ a road test to get a license.

3. You _____ to carry your license with you at all times when you drive.

4. You _____ all traffic signs. They are there for a reason!

5. When you see a stop sign, you _____. Don't just slow down.

6. You _____ faster than the maximum speed limit.

7. You _____ lanes without signaling.

8. When it's dark, you _____ your headlights.

9. You _____ the scene of an accident. Wait until the police arrive.

10. In most countries, the driver and passengers _____ seat belts.

11. In some places, you _____ on a cell phone unless you have a headset. Make sure you know the local laws.

12. Small children _____ in a special safety seat.

13. Alcohol and driving don't mix. You _____ absolutely never _____ and drive.

14. Driving regulations differ from country to country. You _____ the rules before you take to the road in a foreign country!

EXERCISE 2 AFFIRMATIVE AND NEGATIVE STATEMENTS WITH *HAVE TO*

Read about driving rules in different countries. Complete the statements with the correct affirmative or negative form of *have to* and the verbs in parentheses.

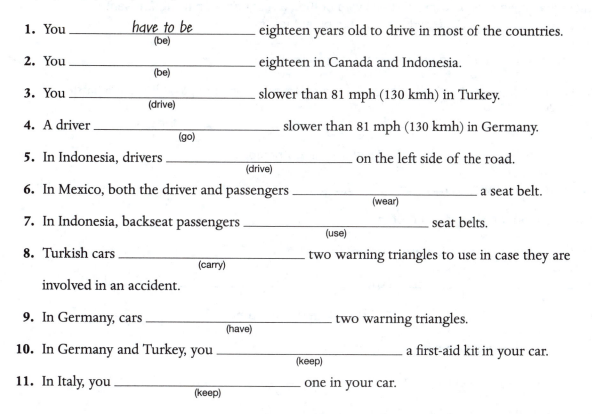

	Minimum driving age	Maximum speed limit on major highway	Side of road	Seat belt law	Warning triangle	First-aid kit
Canada	16	62 mph/ 100 kmh*	right	driver and passengers	no	no
Germany	18	none	right	driver and passengers	yes (1)	yes
Indonesia	17	62 mph/ 100 kmh	left	driver and front seat passenger	yes (1)	yes
Italy	18	81 mph/ 130 kmh	right	driver and passengers	yes (1)	recommended
Mexico	18	68 mph/ 110 kmh	right	driver and passengers	no	no
Turkey	18	74 mph/ 120 kmh	right	driver and passengers	yes (2)	yes

*depends on the part of the country

1. You _____*have to be*_____ eighteen years old to drive in most of the countries.
   (be)

2. You _____ eighteen in Canada and Indonesia.
   (be)

3. You _____ slower than 81 mph (130 kmh) in Turkey.
   (drive)

4. A driver _____ slower than 81 mph (130 kmh) in Germany.
   (go)

5. In Indonesia, drivers _____ on the left side of the road.
   (drive)

6. In Mexico, both the driver and passengers _____ a seat belt.
   (wear)

7. In Indonesia, backseat passengers _____ seat belts.
   (use)

8. Turkish cars _____ two warning triangles to use in case they are involved in an accident.
   (carry)

9. In Germany, cars _____ two warning triangles.
   (have)

10. In Germany and Turkey, you _____ a first-aid kit in your car.
    (keep)

11. In Italy, you _____ one in your car.
    (keep)

EXERCISE 3 CONTRAST: *MUST NOT* OR *NOT HAVE TO*

Look at the chart in Exercise 2 on page 173. Complete the statements with *must not* or the correct form of *not have to*.

1. If you are under the age of eighteen, you _____*must not*_____ drive in most of the countries listed in the chart.

2. You _____ be eighteen to drive in Canada.

3. You _____ obey a speed limit on major German highways.

4. In Turkey, you _____ drive on the left side of the road.

5. In Mexico, drivers _____ carry a warning triangle.

6. In Indonesia, passengers in the back seat _____ wear seat belts.

7. You _____ drive without a first-aid kit in Germany and Turkey.

8. You _____ have a first-aid kit in Italy.

EXERCISE 4 STATEMENTS, QUESTIONS, AND SHORT ANSWERS WITH *HAVE TO*

Complete the conversations with short answers or the correct form of *have to* (present, past, future, or present perfect) and the verbs in parentheses.

1. A: Did you pass your road test the first time you took it?

   B: No. I _____*had to take*_____ it two more times before I passed! What a hassle!
   (take)

2. A: _____ we _____ for gas?
   (stop)

   B: _____. The tank's almost empty.

3. A: How many times _____ you _____ public
   (use)

   transportation since you moved here?

   B: Only once. When my car broke down.

4. A: _____ you _____ late yesterday?
   (work)

   B: _____. Luckily, I finished on time.

5. A: Are you thinking of buying a new car?

   B: Not yet. But in a couple of years, I _____ another one.
   (get)

6. A: Why didn't you come to the meeting last night?

   B: I _____ my uncle to the airport.
   (drive)

7. **A:** My wife got a speeding ticket last week. She was really annoyed. She was only going five miles above the speed limit.

   B: Really? How much _____ she _____?
   (pay)

   A: It was more than $100. They've gotten very strict about enforcing speed limits.

8. **A:** _____ your son ever _____ for a traffic
   (pay)
   violation?

   B: _____. He's a very careful driver.

9. **A:** _____ I _____ a new license when I move?
   (get)

   B: _____. You can only use an out-of-state license for 10 days.

10. **A:** Do you have car insurance?

    B: Of course. Everyone in this country _____ car insurance.
    (have)

11. **A:** How often _____ you _____ your car
    (get)
    inspected in your state?

    B: Every two years.

EXERCISE 5 CONTRAST: *MUST, MUST NOT, HAVE TO,* AND *CAN'T*

Read the online test questions about road signs in the United States. Fill in the circle next to the correct answer.

1. When you see [YIELD] it means:

   ◯ You must come to a complete stop.
   ◯ You must not stop.
   ● You don't have to stop, but you must slow down and prepare to stop if necessary.

2. When you see [STOP] it means:

   ◯ You don't have to stop.
   ◯ You must stop.
   ◯ You can't stop.

(continued on next page)

3. When you see SPEED LIMIT 50 it means:

- ◯ You must drive 50 miles per hour.
- ◯ You must not drive faster than 50 miles per hour.
- ◯ You don't have to drive more than 50 miles per hour.

4. When you see NO TURN ON RED it means:

- ◯ You have to turn when the light is red.
- ◯ You don't have to turn when the light is red.
- ◯ You must not turn when the light is red.

5. When you see DO NOT ENTER it means:

- ◯ You must not enter.
- ◯ You don't have to enter.
- ◯ You must enter.

6. When you see DO NOT PASS it means:

- ◯ You don't have to pass another car.
- ◯ You can't pass another car.
- ◯ You have to pass another car.

7. When you see ONE WAY it means:

- ◯ You must drive in the direction of the arrow.
- ◯ You must not drive in the direction of the arrow.
- ◯ You don't have to drive in the direction of the arrow.

8. When you see MAXIMUM SPEED 65 MINIMUM SPEED 45 it means:

- ◯ You have to drive 45 miles per hour or slower.
- ◯ You can't drive 70 miles per hour.
- ◯ You don't have to drive 70 miles per hour.

9. When you see NO LEFT TURN it means:

- ◯ You must turn left.
- ◯ You can't turn left.
- ◯ You don't have to turn right.

10. When you see NO PARKING 8:30a.m. TO 5:30p.m. it means:

- ◯ You can't park at 5:00 a.m.
- ◯ You must not park at 7:00 p.m.
- ◯ You don't have to move your car at 6:00 p.m.

EXERCISE 6 EDITING

Read the email. There are eight mistakes in expressing necessity. The first mistake is already corrected. Find and correct seven more.

Hi Jason!

Sorry I haven't written before, but there are so many things I've ~~must~~ had to do since we moved

to California. For one, I have to taking a driving test. My brother is lucky. He must not

take one because he got a license when he was a student here. And you really have to

drive if you live here—it's very hard to get around without a car! So, I've been studying

the Driver Handbook, and I've found some pretty interesting—and sometimes

strange—things:

• You can't smoke when a minor (that's someone under the age of eighteen) is in the car.

• You can use a cell phone, but you has got to use one with a hands-free device.

• You must no "dump or abandon animals on a highway." (I can't imagine anyone doing

  this, can you?) If you do, you will probably must pay a fine of $1,000, or go to jail for

  six months, or both!

Did you must take a road test when you moved to Italy?

I've got go now. Let me hear from you!

R.

EXERCISE 7 PERSONAL WRITING

Write a paragraph about a time you moved. What did you have to do? What didn't you have to do? Use the ideas from the box and your own ideas.

buy furniture	learn to drive
find a place to live	make new friends
learn a new language	paint

EXAMPLE: Moving is difficult. There are so many things you have to do. When I first came to this country, I stayed with my aunt and uncle. That was good because I didn't have to find an apartment right away. There were, however, many other things that I had to do. I had to . . .

_____

_____

_____

_____

_____

_____

_____

_____

_____

_____

30 Expectations: *Be supposed to*

EXERCISE 1 AFFIRMATIVE AND NEGATIVE STATEMENTS WITH *BE SUPPOSED TO*

Today, in some countries, when people get married, the groom's family often shares the expenses, and older couples often pay for their own weddings. However, some people are still traditional. Read the chart and complete the sentences with a form of *be supposed to*.

TRADITIONAL WEDDING ETIQUETTE: WHO DOES WHAT	
Role of the Bride's Family	**Role of the Groom's Family**
send invitations pay for food supply flowers pay for the groom's ring provide music	pay for the bride's ring give a rehearsal dinner[1] pay for the honeymoon[2] provide beverages

[1] *rehearsal dinner:* a dinner that usually takes place the night before the wedding ceremony, attended by the bride, the groom, people who will be part of the ceremony, and often out-of-town guests
[2] *honeymoon:* a vacation by two people who just got married

1. The groom's family _____*isn't supposed to send*_____ the invitations.

2. The bride's family _____ the invitations.

3. The bride's parents _____ the music.

4. The groom's parents _____ the music.

5. The groom's family _____ the groom's ring.

6. The groom's family _____ the bride's ring.

7. The bride's parents _____ the honeymoon.

8. The groom's family _____ the honeymoon.

9. The bride's parents _____ the rehearsal dinner.

10. The groom's parents _____ the rehearsal dinner.

11. The groom's family _____ the flowers.

12. The bride's family _____ the food.

13. The groom's family _____ the beverages.

EXERCISE 2 AFFIRMATIVE AND NEGATIVE STATEMENTS WITH *BE SUPPOSED TO*

Erica Nelson is getting married. She completed this change-of-address form, but she made eight mistakes. Find the mistakes and write sentences with *was supposed to* and *wasn't supposed to*. Include the number of the item that has the mistake.

U.S. Postal Service **CHANGE OF ADDRESS ORDER**	Customer Instructions: Complete Items 1 thru 9, Except Item 8, please PRINT all information including address on face of card.	**OFFICIAL USE ONLY**

| 1. Change of address for *(Check one)* | ☑ Individual ☑ Entire Family ☐ Business | Zone/Route Id No. |

2. Start Date: Month `3 0` Day `0 6` Year `9 5`

3. If TEMPORARY address, print date to discontinue forwarding: Month ___ Day ___ Year ___

Date Entered on Form 3982: M M D D Y Y

Expiration Date: M M D D Y Y

Clerk/Carrier Endorsements

4. Print Last Name or Name of Business *(If more than one use, use separate Change of Address Order Form for each)*
`E R I C A`

5. Print First Name of Head of Household (include Jr., Sr., etc.). Leave Blank if the Change of Address Order is for a business.
`N E L S O N`

6. Print OLD mailing address, number and street *(if Puerto Rico, include urbanization zone)*
`2 6   M A P L E   R O A D`

Apt./Suite No. `4 A`   P.O. Box No.   R.R/HCR No.   Rural Box/HCR Box No.

City `B O S T O N`   State `M A`   Zip Code `–`

7. Print NEW Mailing address, number and street *(if Puerto Rico, include urbanization zone)*
`2 9 8 7   C O S B Y   A V E`

Apt./Suite No.   P.O. Box No.   R.R/HCR No.   Rural Box/HCR Box No.

City `A M H E R S T`   State   Zip Code `–`

8. Signature *(See conditions on reverse)*   **OFFICIAL USE ONLY**
Erica Nelson

9. Date Signed: Month ___ Day ___ Year ___

OFFICIAL USE ONLY

Verification Endorsement

PS Form 3575, June 2016 ☆ U.S.G.P.O. 2016-309-315

1. Item __1__ *She was supposed to check one box.* OR *She wasn't supposed to check two boxes.*

2. Item ____ _____

3. Item ____ _____

4. Item ____ _____

5. Item ____ _____

6. Item ____ _____

7. Item ____ _____

8. Item ____ _____

EXERCISE 3 QUESTIONS AND ANSWERS WITH *BE SUPPOSED TO*

Erica and Adam are on their honeymoon. Complete the conversations. Use the words from the box and *be supposed to*. Use short answers when necessary.

~~arrive~~	call	get	leave	shake
be	do	land	rain	tip

1. ERICA: What time _____are_____ we _____supposed to arrive_____ in Bermuda?

    ADAM: Well, the plane _____ at 10:30, but it looks like we're going to be

    a little late.

2. ERICA: What time _____ we _____ to the hotel?

    ADAM: Check-in time is 12:00.

3. ERICA: _____ we _____ if we're going to be late?

    ADAM: _____. We'd better call as soon as we land.

4. ADAM: How much _____ we _____ the person who carries our bags

    for us?

    ERICA: I think it's $1.00 a bag.

5. ADAM: _____ the hotel restaurant _____ good?

    ERICA: _____. The travel agent suggested that we go somewhere else for

    a nice dinner.

6. ERICA: What _____ we _____ with our keys when we leave the hotel?

    Can we take them with us?

    ADAM: We _____ them at the front desk.

7. ERICA: _____ it _____ today?

    ADAM: No, _____. But look at those clouds. I think we'd better take an

    umbrella just in case.

8. ERICA: Can you hand me that bottle of sunblock?

    ADAM: Sure. _____ you _____ the bottle before you use it?

    ERICA: I don't know. What do the instructions say?

EXERCISE 4 AFFIRMATIVE AND NEGATIVE STATEMENTS WITH *BE SUPPOSED TO*

Plans change! Read about Erica and Adam's plans. Write two statements for each item—one affirmative, the other negative. Sometimes you will begin with an affirmative statement, other times you will begin with a negative statement. Use the correct form of *be supposed to*.

1. Erica planned to be a doctor, but she became a lawyer instead.

   A: *Erica was supposed to be a doctor.*

   B: *She wasn't supposed to become a lawyer.*

2. Adam didn't plan to become an engineer. He wanted to be an architect.

   A: _____

   B: _____

3. Erica and Adam planned to get married in June, but they got married in September.

   A: _____

   B: _____

4. They didn't plan to have a big wedding. They expected to have a small one.

   A: _____

   B: _____

5. They wanted a short ceremony, but it was long.

   A: _____

   B: _____

6. They planned to go to London for their honeymoon, but they went to Bermuda instead.

   A: _____

   B: _____

7. They planned to live in Boston, but they moved to Amherst.

   A: _____

   B: _____

8. They didn't plan to rent an apartment. They planned to buy a house.

   A: _____

   B: _____

EXERCISE 5 EDITING

Read Erica's postcard. There are six mistakes in the use of *be supposed to*. The first mistake is already corrected. Find and correct five more.

Here we are in beautiful Bermuda. It's sunny, 80°F, and ~~it will~~ *it's*
supposed to get even warmer later today.

I'm so glad we decided to come here for our honeymoon. We was supposed to go to
London, but we decided we really needed a relaxing beach vacation instead. The hotel is
very nice. We were supposed to get a standard double room, but when they found out we
were on our honeymoon, they upgraded us to a suite with an ocean view. Tonight we're
eating at Chez Marcel's. It supposes to be one of the best restaurants on the island.

Gotta go now. I suppose to meet Adam in a few minutes. He's supposed to join me at the
beach, but decided to play some tennis instead.

Thanks for offering to pick us up at the airport. We're supposed to arriving at 5:30 p.m.,
but check with the airport before to see if there are any delays. See you soon!

Love,

Erica

EXERCISE 6 PERSONAL WRITING

Everyone makes plans, but plans often change. Write a paragraph about your own changed plans. Use *was / were* and *wasn't / weren't supposed to.*

EXAMPLE: Three years ago I was supposed to move to California, but my plans changed. My father got a job in Texas, and so my family and I moved here instead. We were supposed to . . .

_____

_____

_____

_____

_____

_____

_____

_____

_____

_____

_____

Future Possibility: *May, Might, Could*

EXERCISE 1 AFFIRMATIVE AND NEGATIVE STATEMENTS

Read Lauren's journal entry. Complete the sentences with the words in parentheses.
Choose between affirmative and negative.

Thursday, July 3

I was supposed to go to the beach tomorrow, but the weather forecast says it

_____**might rain**_____. I'm not really sure what I'll do if it rains. I think
1. (might / rain)

I _____ shopping at the mall instead. It's a holiday
2. (may / go)

weekend, so there _____ some good sales. I really need
3. (could / be)

some new clothes. I _____ find a dress for John's party.
4. (might / be able to)

Maybe I'll call Julie. She _____ to go with me. That would
5. (might / want)

be great. She always knows the latest clothing trends.

On second thought, shopping _____ such a good idea.
6. (may / be)

The stores will probably be really crowded. I _____ to a
7. (could / go)

movie instead. There's a Spanish film at the local movie theater, but I'm a little

afraid that I _____ enough of it. My Spanish really isn't
8. (might / understand)

that good. Maybe I'll call Eric and ask him if he wants to take a drive to see Aunt

Marla and Uncle Phil. He _____ to go, though, because he
9. (might / want)

doesn't like driving in the rain. It's crazy how much the weather affects people's

plans. Oh, well. I _____ home and read a good book. That
10. (could / stay)

_____ the best thing to do.
11. (might / be)

EXERCISE 2 CONTRAST: *BE GOING TO* OR *MIGHT*

Read the conversations. Use *be going to* or *might* and the verbs from the box to complete the summary sentences.

buy	go	rain	see	work
call	have	read	~~visit~~	write

1. **LAUREN:** Hello, Julie? This is Lauren. Do you want to go to the mall with me?

   JULIE: I don't know. I'm thinking about going to my parents'.

   SUMMARY: Julie _____*might visit*_____ her parents.

2. **JULIE:** What are you looking for at the mall?

   LAUREN: I need to get a new dress for John's party.

   JULIE: Good luck! I hope you find something.

   SUMMARY: Lauren _____ a new dress.

3. **LAUREN:** Do you think we'll get some rain?

   CARL: Definitely. Look at those clouds.

   SUMMARY: Carl thinks it _____.

4. **LAUREN:** What are you doing today?

   CARL: I have tickets for a play.

   SUMMARY: Carl _____ a play.

5. **LAUREN:** What are you doing this weekend?

   KAYLA: I'm not sure. I'm thinking about taking a drive to the country.

   SUMMARY: Kayla _____ for a ride.

6. **LAUREN:** Say, Eric. Do you want to see Aunt Marla and Uncle Phil tomorrow?

   ERIC: I can't. I have to go into the office this weekend—even though it's a holiday.

   SUMMARY: Eric _____ this weekend.

7. **LAUREN:** How about dinner Saturday night?

   ERIC: That's an idea. Can I call and let you know tomorrow?

   LAUREN: Sure.

   SUMMARY: Lauren and Eric _____ dinner together.

8. LAUREN: Hi, Aunt Marla. How are you?

MARLA: Lauren! How are you? It's good to hear your voice. Listen, we just started dinner. Can I call you back?

LAUREN: Sure.

MARLA: OK. I'll speak to you later.

SUMMARY: Marla _____ Lauren later.

9. MARLA: Hi. It's Aunt Marla. Sorry about before. What are you doing home on a holiday weekend? Why aren't you out?

LAUREN: I'm tired. I just want to stay home with a good book.

SUMMARY: Lauren _____ a book.

10. MARLA: Do you have any other plans?

LAUREN: Maybe I'll catch up on some of my emails.

SUMMARY: Lauren _____ some emails.

EXERCISE 3 EDITING

Read Lauren's email. There are five mistakes in the use of modals to express future possibility. The first mistake is already corrected. Find and correct four more.

> Hi Rachel,
>
> How are you? It's the Fourth of July, and it's raining really hard. They say it could ~~cleared~~ *clear* up later. Then again, it could not. You never know with the weather.
>
> Do you remember my brother, Eric? He says hi. He might has dinner with me on Saturday night. We may go to a new Mexican restaurant that just opened in the mall.
>
> I definitely might take some vacation time next month. Perhaps we could do something together. It might not be fun to do some traveling. What do you think? Let me know.
>
> Lauren

EXERCISE 4 PERSONAL WRITING

A. Make a short "To Do" list for next weekend. Put a question mark (?) next to the things you aren't sure you'll do.

To Do
1.
2.
3.
4.
5.
6.
7.
8.

B. Now write a paragraph about what you *are going to do* and what you *might do*.

EXAMPLE: I have a lot of plans for next weekend, but I know I won't be able to do everything. I'm definitely going to watch the football game with Tom and Lisa, but I might not have time to finish painting the kitchen . . .

_____

_____

_____

_____

_____

_____

_____

_____

_____

_____

Present Conclusions: *Must, Have (got) to, May, Might, Could, Can't*

EXERCISE 1 AFFIRMATIVE AND NEGATIVE STATEMENTS WITH *MUST*

Read the facts. Complete the conclusions with *must* or *must not*.

1. Jack is wearing a gold wedding band on his ring finger.

   CONCLUSION: He _____ *must be* _____ married.
   (be)

2. You have been calling Alicia since 8:00 p.m., but no one answers the phone.

   CONCLUSION: She _____ home.
   (be)

3. Christa got 98 percent on her math test.

   CONCLUSION: Her parents _____ proud of her.
   (feel)

4. Carlos works from 9:00 to 5:00 and then attends night school.

   CONCLUSION: He _____ a lot of free time.
   (have)

5. Martin works as a mechanic in Al's Automobile Shop.

   CONCLUSION: He _____ a lot about cars.
   (know)

6. Monica owns two houses and four cars.

   CONCLUSION: She _____ a lot of money.
   (have)

7. Mr. Cantor always asks me to repeat what I say.

   CONCLUSION: He _____ well.
   (hear)

8. Chen got only four hours of sleep last night.

   CONCLUSION: He _____ very tired today.
   (feel)

9. Tyrone has been at R & L, Inc. for more than 20 years.

   CONCLUSION: He _____ a good position there.
   (have)

10. This job advertisement doesn't mention the salary.

    CONCLUSION: That's not a good sign. It _____ very good!
    (be)

11. Carmen was born in Mexico and moved to the United States when she was ten.

    CONCLUSION: She _____ Spanish.
    (speak)

(continued on next page)

12. Mindy never gets good grades.

CONCLUSION: She _____ enough.
(study)

13. Dan just bought a bottle of aspirin and four boxes of tissues.

CONCLUSION: He _____ a cold.
(have)

14. Ana and Giorgio didn't have any of the steak.

CONCLUSION: They _____ meat.
(eat)

15. Detective Menendez solves a lot of crimes.

CONCLUSION: His methods _____ very effective.
(be)

EXERCISE 2 CONTRAST: *MUST* OR *MAY / MIGHT / COULD*

Read the conversations. Circle the appropriate words.

1. A: Someone broke into the Petersons' house.

B: That's terrible! What did they take?

A: All of Mrs. Peterson's jewelry.

B: Oh, no. She could / (must) feel awful.

A: Is she home now? I'd like to call her.

B: I don't know. She might / must be home. She sometimes gets home by 6:00.

2. A: Do the Petersons have insurance?

B: Oh, they could / must. Mr. Peterson works at an insurance company.

3. A: Have you checked our burglar alarm lately?

B: Yes. And I just put in a new battery.

A: Good. So it must / might be OK.

4. A: Do you remember that guy we saw outside the Petersons' home last week?

B: Yes. Why? Do you think he might / must be the burglar?

A: I don't know. I guess he must / could be the burglar. He looked a little suspicious.

B: Maybe we should tell the police about him.

A: Maybe.

5. A: Someone's at the door.

   B: Who <u>could / must</u> it be?

   A: I don't know.

   B: Detective Menendez wanted to ask us some questions about the burglary.

   A: Oh. It <u>must / could</u> be him. We're not expecting anybody else.

6. A: How old do you think Detective Menendez is?

   B: Well, he's been a detective for ten years. So he <u>must / might</u> be at least thirty-five.

   A: You're right. He <u>couldn't / might not</u> be much younger than thirty-five. He probably started out as a police officer and became a detective in his mid-twenties.

   B: He looks a lot younger, though.

EXERCISE 3 SHORT ANSWERS WITH *MUST* OR *MAY, MIGHT, COULD*

Write a short answer to each question. Use *must, may, might,* or *could* and include *be* where necessary.

1. A: Is Ron a reporter?

   B: _____ *He might be* _____. He always carries a notepad and asks a lot of questions.

2. A: Does Marta speak Spanish?

   B: _____. She lived in Spain for fifteen years.

3. A: Do the Taylors have a lot of money?

   B: _____.They're always taking very expensive vacations.

4. A: Is Ricardo married?

   B: _____. He wears a wedding ring.

5. A: Does Anna know Meng?

   B: _____. They both work for the same company, but it's very big.

6. A: Is your phone out of order?

   B: _____. It hasn't rung once today, and John always calls me by this time.

7. A: Is that online encyclopedia any good?

   B: _____. It's *very* popular.

(continued on next page)

8. A: Are Marcia and Scott married?

   B: _____. They both have the same last name, but it's possible that

   they're brother and sister.

9. A: Does Glenda drive?

   B: _____. She owns a car.

10. A: Is Oscar an only child?

    B: _____. I don't know. He's never mentioned a brother or sister.

11. A: Are the Hendersons away?

    B: _____. I haven't seen them for a week, and there are no lights on in

    their apartment.

EXERCISE 4 CONTRAST: *MIGHT, MUST, COULD, CAN'T, COULDN'T, MIGHT NOT*

Read the description of a burglary suspect and look at the four pictures. Complete the conversation with the correct words and the names of the men in the pictures.

21-year-old white male

short, curly blond hair

no scars or other

distinguishing features

Allen

Bob

Chet

Dave

DETECTIVE: Please look at these four photos. It's possible that one of these men

_____ be the man we're looking for. Take your time.
       _____*could*_____
       1. (must / could)

WITNESS 1: Hmmm. What do you think? _____ it be this man?
                              2. (could / must)

WITNESS 2: It _____ be _____. He has a scar on his
3. (can't / must)   4. (name)

face. What about _____? He has short blond hair and looks like
5. (name)

he's twenty-one.

WITNESS 1: I'm not sure. It _____ be. But it _____
6. (could / must)   7. (might / must)

also be _____. He also has blond hair and looks twenty-one.
8. (name)

WITNESS 2: But he has long hair.

WITNESS 1: The photo _____ be old. Maybe he cut it.
9. (could / couldn't)

WITNESS 2: That's true. Well, it definitely _____ be
10. (couldn't / might not)

_____. He looks too old. I don't know. Maybe we could look at
11. (name)

some more photos.

EXERCISE 5 EDITING

Read the email from one of the witnesses. There are five mistakes in the use of modals to express conclusions. The first mistake is already corrected. Find and correct four more.

● ● ●

                                                      must
Just got home. It's really cold outside. The temperature ~~could~~ be below freezing because the

walkway is all covered with ice. What a day! We went down to the police station to look at

photos. I was amazed. They must having hundreds of photos. They kept showing us more and

more. We kept looking, but it was difficult to be sure. After all, we only saw the burglar for a few

seconds. They've got to have other witnesses besides us! There were a lot of people at the mall

that day. We may not be the only ones who got a look at the burglar! That's the one thing I'm

certain of! In spite of our uncertainty with the photos, the detective was very patient. I guess he

must be used to witnesses like us. Nevertheless, it have to be frustrating for him. I know the

police may really want to catch this guy!

EXERCISE 6 PERSONAL WRITING

Read the description of the burglar in Exercise 4 on page 192. Look at the pictures. Is one of them the burglar? What's your opinion? Write a paragraph. Use *must be, has (got) to be, could be, might be, may be, couldn't be,* and *can't be*. Give reasons for your opinions.

Ed   Frank   George

EXAMPLE: It isn't always easy to identify someone. Is one of these men the burglar? It couldn't be . . . because . . .

_____

_____

_____

_____

_____

_____

_____

_____

_____

_____

_____

_____

Workbook Answer Key

EXERCISE 1

2. coming, comes
3. doing, does
4. getting, gets
5. going, goes
6. having, has
7. living, lives
8. looking, looks
9. meeting, meets
10. planning, plans
11. playing, plays
12. reading, reads
13. running, runs
14. saying, says
15. starting, starts
16. studying, studies
17. taking, takes
18. watching, watches
19. working, works
20. writing, writes

EXERCISE 2

2. is walking
3. isn't wearing
4. doesn't look
5. likes
6. doesn't understand
7. is
8. 's looking
9. 's getting
10. thinks
11. is
12. come
13. act

EXERCISE 3

Postcard A
2. 'm standing
3. is getting
4. looks
5. rains
6. has
7. 's taking
8. 's starting

Postcard B
1. love
2. 'm studying
3. living
4. is improving
5. speak
6. means
7. 're helping
8. want
9. miss

EXERCISE 4

3. Aldo and Emilia (OR They) go to school.
4. Aldo and Emilia (OR They) are having lunch.
5. Aldo works at the bookstore. Emilia studies at the library.
6. Aldo plays soccer. Emilia plays basketball.
7. Aldo is going home. Emilia is doing homework at the library.
8. Aldo has dinner. Emilia practices the guitar.
9. Aldo does homework. Emilia has dinner.
10. Aldo is playing computer games. Emilia is watching TV.

EXERCISE 5

2. Aldo doesn't watch TV. He reads the newspaper.
3. Emilia doesn't work at the bookstore. Aldo works at the bookstore. (OR She studies at the library.)
4. Emilia isn't playing tennis. She's playing basketball.
5. They don't always have dinner together. Aldo has dinner at 6:00. Emilia has dinner at 7:00.

EXERCISE 6

2. A: When do Aldo and Emilia get up?
   B: They get up at 7:30.
3. A: Does Emilia walk in the morning?
   B: No, she doesn't.
4. A: What are they doing now?
   B: They're having lunch.
5. A: Is Aldo doing homework now?
   B: No, he isn't.
6. A: Does Emilia do her homework at school?
   B: No, she doesn't.
7. A: When does Emilia play basketball?
   B: (She plays basketball) at 4:00.
8. A: Does Aldo play computer games before dinner?
   B: No, he doesn't.

EXERCISE 7

2. Emilia is usually on time. OR Usually Emilia is on time.
3. Aldo and Emilia never miss school.
4. These days they're studying English. OR They're studying English these days.
5. They usually speak Italian. OR Usually they speak Italian.
6. Now they're speaking English. OR They're speaking English now.
7. Aldo and Emilia always do their homework.
8. Aldo is often tired.
9. The students usually eat lunch in school. OR Usually the students eat lunch in school.
10. They're always hungry.
11. At the moment, Emilia is having a snack. OR Emilia is having a snack at the moment.
12. Emilia rarely goes to bed late.

EXERCISE 8

How are you? ~~I write~~ *I'm writing* you this email before my class.
~~I'm having~~ *have* a part-time job as a clerk in the mailroom
of a small company. The pay isn't good, but ~~I'm liking~~ *I like*

the people there. They're all friendly, and we ~~are~~ *speak* ~~speaking~~ Spanish all the time. I'm also taking classes at

night school. I'm studying the language and culture of

this country. The class *meets* ~~is meeting~~ three times a week. It

just started last week, so *I don't know* ~~I'm not knowing~~ many of the

other students yet. They seem nice, though.

I think ~~I'm thinking~~ that I'm beginning to get accustomed

to living here. At first, I experienced some "culture

shock." I understand that this is quite normal. But these

days *I'm meeting* ~~I meet~~ more and more people because of my job

and my class, so I'm feeling more connected to things.

I'm also having fewer misunderstandings because of the

language.

What *are you doing* ~~do you do~~ these days? *Are you still looking* ~~Do you still look~~ for a

new job?

Please write when you can. *I always like* ~~I'm always liking~~ to hear

from you.

EXERCISE 9

Answers will vary.

UNIT 2 Simple Past

EXERCISE 1

2. began
3. bought
4. caught
5. came
6. died
7. did
8. felt
9. found
10. got
11. gave
12. had
13. hurried
14. kissed
15. lived
16. looked
17. met
18. moved
19. needed
20. opened
21. put
22. read
23. said
24. saw
25. took
26. thought
27. understood
28. voted
29. won
30. wrote
31. was, were

EXERCISE 2

2. wasn't
3. weren't, were
4. wasn't
5. was
6. wasn't, was
7. was, wasn't
8. wasn't, was
9. were
10. were

EXERCISE 3

2. **A:** Where was Simone de Beauvoir from?
   B: She was from France.
3. **A:** What nationality was Pablo Neruda?
   B: He was Chilean.
4. **A:** Who was Wang Wei?
   B: He was a (Chinese) poet, musician, and painter.
5. **A:** Was Agatha Christie French?
   B: No, she wasn't.
6. **A:** What nationality was Lucy M. Montgomery?
   B: She was Canadian.
7. **A:** Was Nâzim Hikmet a poet?
   B: Yes, he was.
8. **A:** When was Karel Čapek born?
   B: He was born in 1890.

EXERCISE 4

Biography A
2. grew up
3. taught
4. began
5. loved
6. used
7. wrote
8. moved
9. died

Biography B
1. was
2. planned
3. began
4. painted
5. studied
6. taught
7. loved
8. married
9. had
10. died

Biography C
1. were
2. went
3. built
4. flew
5. watched
6. took place
7. lasted

EXERCISE 5

2. **A:** Where did he grow up?
   B: He grew up in Hungary.
3. **A:** What did he do?
   B: He was a composer. OR He wrote music.
4. **A:** Did he spend his whole life in Hungary?
   B: No, he didn't.
5. **A:** Did Frida Kahlo plan to be a painter?
   B: No, she didn't.
6. **A:** When did she begin painting?
   B: She began painting after a serious accident.
7. **A:** What did she paint?
   B: She painted (pictures of) her family and friends. She also painted pictures of herself.
8. **A:** When did she die?
   B: She died in 1954.
9. **A:** Where did the Wright brothers build their first planes?
   B: (They built their first planes) in their bicycle shop in Ohio.

10. A: Did both brothers fly the *Flyer 1*?
B: No, they didn't.

11. A: Where did the first controlled flight take place?
B: (It took place) near Kitty Hawk, North Carolina.

12. A: How long did the flight last?
B: (It lasted) only about 12 seconds.

EXERCISE 6

3. Orville didn't have serious health problems.
4. Wilbur didn't grow a moustache.
5. Orville didn't lose most of his hair.
6. Wilbur didn't take courses in Latin.
7. Wilbur didn't like to play jokes.
8. Wilbur didn't dress very fashionably.
9. Wilbur didn't play the guitar.
10. Orville didn't build the first glider.
11. Orville didn't make the first attempts to fly.
12. Orville didn't choose the location of Kitty Hawk.
13. Wilbur didn't have a lot of patience.
14. Wilbur didn't live a long life.

EXERCISE 7

Pablo Neruda (1904–1973) ~~were~~ *was* a famous poet,
political activist, and ambassador. He was born in Parral,
Chile. His mother, a school teacher, ~~dies~~ *died* just two months
after Neruda's birth. His father ~~work~~ *worked* for the railroad.
He ~~no~~ *did not* support Neruda's early interest in writing. He
wanted him to do something more "practical." When he
was seventeen, Neruda ~~gone~~ *went* to Santiago to continue his
education. At first, he planned to become a teacher like
his mother, but soon he ~~beginned~~ *began* to write poems. He
did not ~~finished~~ *finish* school, but he published his first book of
poetry before he ~~were~~ *was* twenty. In one of his love poems,
he ~~describe~~ *described* "restless rocks" at the bottom of the ocean.
Like the rocks in his poem, Neruda did not ~~stayed~~ *stay* in one
place. He ~~spends~~ *spent* decades traveling and writing poetry.
His poems ~~did show~~ *showed* strong emotions and beautiful
imagery. In 1971, while he was Chile's ambassador to
France, he ~~winned~~ *won* the Nobel Prize in literature. Neruda
~~dead~~ *died* two years later.

EXERCISE 8

Answers will vary.

UNIT 3 Past Progressive and Simple Past

EXERCISE 1

2. wasn't writing
3. was answering
4. were eating
5. weren't eating
6. weren't discussing
7. were discussing
8. wasn't answering
9. was returning
10. was attending

EXERCISE 2

2. A: What was he doing at 9:30?
B: He was meeting with Ms. Jacobs.

3. A: Was Mr. Cotter writing police reports at 10:30?
B: No, he wasn't.

4. A: What kind of reports was he writing?
B: He was writing financial reports.

5. A: What was he doing at 11:30?
B: He was answering correspondence.

6. A: Was he having lunch at 12:00?
B: Yes, he was.

7. A: Who was eating lunch with him?
B: Mr. Webb was eating lunch with him.

8. A: Where were they having lunch?
B: They were having lunch at Sol's Café.

9. A: Who was he talking to at 3:30?
B: He was talking to Alan.

EXERCISE 3

2. was crossing
3. was speeding
4. didn't stop
5. was
6. saw
7. was walking
8. saw
9. noticed
10. was going
11. reached
12. went
13. hit
14. took out
15. called
16. didn't stop
17. happened
18. came
19. got
20. was lying
21. was bleeding
22. was
23. were questioning
24. said
25. was crossing
26. went
27. knocked
28. happened
29. had
30. was crossing
31. didn't see
32. broke
33. had
34. were not

EXERCISE 4

2. What did you do when you heard the noise?
3. What did you see when you looked in the direction of the sound?
4. Where were you standing when you saw the Honda?
5. Did the driver stop when the accident occurred?
6. What happened next?

7. Did you get a look at the driver while he was driving away?

8. What was the victim doing when the car hit her?

EXERCISE 5

    LONDON, June 31, 2009—Millvina Dean, the last
survivor of the 1912 *Titanic* disaster, ~~was dying~~ ^{died} yesterday
in Southampton, England. She was 97.

    Dean had no memories of the disaster. She was
only two months old when she and her family were
passengers on the luxury ship's first voyage. The ship
was sailing from Dean's hometown of Southampton,
England, to New York City. On the night of April 14,
they ~~slept~~ ^{were sleeping} in their cabin when the ship hit a huge iceberg.
Dean's father became alarmed and immediately ~~was~~
~~sending~~ ^{sent} his wife and two children to the lifeboats. Dean
~~was believing~~ ^{believed} her father's quick action saved their lives.
Most people thought the ship was unsinkable. "My
father didn't take a chance," she said. Other passengers
weren't as lucky. Just a few hours after the *Titanic* struck
the iceberg, the ship ~~was sinking~~ ^{sank} to the bottom of the
Atlantic. More than 1500 passengers and crew lost their
lives, including Dean's father.

    Dean's family returned to England, where she spent
most of her long life. In her later years, she attended
Titanic conferences and gave interviews. She moved
into a nursing home when she ~~was breaking~~ ^{broke} her hip
three years ago.

    Charles Haas, president of the Titanic International
Society, said that with Dean's death, history lost "the
last living link to the story" of the *Titanic*.

EXERCISE 6
Answers will vary.

UNIT 4 *Used to* and *Would*

EXERCISE 1

2. people used to read
3. people used to cook
4. people used to wash
5. people used to use
6. it used to take

EXERCISE 2

2. used to collect
3. didn't use to have
4. used to take
5. didn't use to be
6. used to live
7. didn't use to like
8. didn't use to know
9. used to make
10. used to return

EXERCISE 3

2. A: Where did she use to live?
    B: She used to live in New York.
3. A: Did she use to live in a house?
    B: No, she didn't.
4. A: What did she use to do?
    B: She used to be a student.
5. A: Which school did she use to attend?
    B: She used to attend City College.
6. A: Did she use to have long hair?
    B: Yes, she did.
7. A: Did she use to wear glasses?
    B: No, she didn't.
8. A: Did she use to be married?
    B: Yes, she did.

EXERCISE 4

2. would get up
3. would go
4. would not get
5. would have to
6. used to be
7. would get around
8. used to look
9. would fly

EXERCISE 5

    Today, I ran into an old classmate. We used to ~~was~~ ^{be}
in the same science class. In fact, we would often study
together for tests. He was a very good student, and he
always would ~~gets~~ ^{get} A's. At first, I almost didn't recognize
Jason! He looked so different. He ~~would have~~ ^{used to have} very dark
hair. Now he's almost all gray. He also used to ~~being~~ ^{be} a
little heavy. Now he's quite thin. And he was wearing a
suit and tie! I couldn't believe it. He never ~~use~~ ^{used} to dress
that way. He only used to ~~wore~~ ^{wear} jeans! His personality
seemed different, too. He didn't use to talk very much.
People didn't dislike him, but he wasn't very popular. In
fact, I really ~~would~~ ^{used to} think he was a little weird. Now he
seems very outgoing. I wonder what he thought of me!
I'm sure I look and act different from the way I ~~was~~

used to, too! I'm really glad we ran into each other. We shared a lot of the same memories. It was awesome!

Maybe we'll see each other again!

EXERCISE 6

Answers will vary.

UNIT 5 Wh- Questions

EXERCISE 1

2. Whose phone rang at midnight?
3. Who was calling for Michelle?
4. Who was having a party?
5. How many people left the party?
6. What surprised them?
7. Whose friend called the police?
8. How many police arrived?
9. What happened next?
10. Who told the police about a theft?
11. Whose jewelry disappeared?
12. How many necklaces vanished?

EXERCISE 2

2. How many rooms does her apartment have? (f)
3. How much rent does she pay? (j)
4. When does she pay the rent? (c)
5. Who does she live with? (h)
6. What does she do? (g)
7. Which company does she work for? (d)
8. How long does she plan to stay there? (a)
9. How does she get to work? (b)
10. Why does she take the bus? (i)

EXERCISE 3

2. Why did you leave Chicago?
3. Who moved with you?
4. Where did you get a job?
5. When did it start?
6. How many rooms does it have?
7. How many of the rooms came with carpeting?
8. How much do you pay (a month)?
9. What do you need to buy?
10. Whose brother wants to visit her?
11. Who called last Sunday?
12. Who else did you speak to?
13. When do they want to visit you?
14. Why is there plenty of room?

EXERCISE 4

Why ∧ the defendant ~~had~~ $10,000 in his wallet? [*did* above ∧, *have* above *had*]

Who gave him the money?

Why did the witness indicate Ms. Rivera?

Where did the defendant ~~met~~ Ms. Rivera? [*meet* above *met*]

~~Who~~ keys did he have? Were they Ms. Rivera's? [*Whose* above *Who*]

Which bus did Ms. Rivera take?

Why ~~she was~~ in a hurry? [*was she* above]

~~Whom~~ saw her on the bus? [*Who* above *Whom*]

What time did she get home?

Why ~~she did~~ look so frightened? [*did she* above]

Who ~~she called~~ when she got home? [*did she call* above]

What ~~did happen~~ next? [*happened* above]

EXERCISE 5

Answers will vary.

PART 2 THE FUTURE
UNIT 6 Future

EXERCISE 1

2. He isn't going to take the train.
   He's going to fly OR take a plane.
3. He isn't going to travel alone.
   He's going to travel with his wife.
4. They aren't going to leave from Chicago.
   They're going to leave from New York City.
5. They aren't going to fly US Airways.
   They're going to fly FairAir.
6. They aren't going to leave on July 11.
   They're going to leave on June 11.
7. They aren't going to take Flight 149.
   They're going to take Flight 194.
8. It isn't going to take off at 7:00 a.m.
   It's going to take off at 7:00 p.m.
9. They aren't going to sit apart.
   They're going to sit together.
10. She isn't going to sit in Seat 15B.
    She's going to sit in Seat 15C.

EXERCISE 2

2. How long are you going to stay?
3. Are you going to stay at a hotel?
4. What are you going to do in San Francisco?
5. Are you going to visit Fisherman's Wharf?
6. Is your daughter going to go with you?
7. What is he going to do?
8. When are you going to leave?

EXERCISE 3

2. will become
3. Will . . . replace
4. won't replace
5. will . . . operate
6. will . . . do
7. 'll be
8. 'll sing
9. 'll dance
10. Will . . . tell
11. will
12. won't . . . be
13. will . . . do
14. Will . . . have
15. will
16. will . . . help
17. 'll replace
18. 'll perform
19. won't be
20. will improve
21. will lose
22. will create
23. Will . . . need
24. will . . . look
25. won't look
26. 'll resemble
27. will . . . happen
28. 'll happen
29. 'll experience

EXERCISE 4

Next Wednesday is the first performance of *Robots* at Town Theater. Melissa Robins is playing the leading role. Robins, who lives in Italy and who is vacationing in Greece, is not available for an interview at this time. She is, however, appearing on Channel 8's *Theater Talk* sometime next month.

Although shows traditionally begin at 8:00 p.m., *Robots*, because of its length, starts half an hour earlier. Immediately following the opening-night performance, the cast is having a reception in the theater lounge. *Robots* was a huge success in London, where all performances quickly sold out, but tickets are still available at Town Theater through March 28th. Call 555–6310 for more information.

EXERCISE 5

2. I'm going to do
3. I'll ask
4. it's going to rain
5. They're showing
6. we're going to have
7. it's going to spill, I'll be
8. I'll take
9. We're going to arrive
10. are we going to get
11. We'll take, will still be
12. We're landing
13. are you going to stay
14. we'll see

EXERCISE 6

2. 're seeing OR 're going to see
3. will . . . need OR are . . . going to need
4. starts
5. 'll get
6. are . . . going to eat OR are . . . eating
7. 're having OR 're going to have
8. are . . . getting OR are . . . going to get OR will . . . get
9. leaves
10. 's going to rain
11. 'll take
12. 'll lie OR 'm going to lie
13. 'll wake
14. is going to be OR will be

EXERCISE 7

I'm going
~~I going~~ to stay here for a week with my parents. Our hotel is incredible, and I spent the afternoon floating in the pool.

we're seeing OR we're going to see
We have a lot of fun things planned. Tonight ~~we'll see~~ a play called Robots. Mom already bought tickets
we're having OR we're going to have
for it. The play begins at 7:30, and before that ~~we have~~ dinner on Fisherman's Wharf. Right now we're still in the hotel, but we'll have to leave soon. It's good that we're going to be indoors most of the time because the
's going to
sky is getting very dark. It ~~will~~ rain!
I'll call
~~I call~~ you soon.

EXERCISE 8

Answers will vary.

UNIT 7 Future Time Clauses

EXERCISE 1

2. gets up . . . 'll take (i)
3. is . . . 'll drink (c)
4. eat . . . 'll read (j)
5. finish . . . 'll do (g)
6. washes . . . 'll dry (e)
7. get in . . . 'll fasten (d)
8. gets . . . 'll drive (b)
9. stops . . . 'll need (f)
10. is . . . 'll be (a)

EXERCISE 2

2. will apply (OR is going to apply) . . . before . . . finishes
3. After . . . finishes . . . 'll visit (OR 's going to visit)
4. While . . . works . . . 'll take (OR 's going to take)
5. 'll visit (OR 's going to visit) . . . before . . . gets
6. When . . . finishes . . . 'll fly (OR 's going to fly)
7. 'll attend (OR 's going to attend) . . . when . . . 's
8. 'll return (OR 's going to return) . . . after . . . attends
9. 'll move (OR 's going to move) . . . when . . . returns
10. After . . . moves . . . will look for (OR is going to look for)

EXERCISE 3

2. . . . Vera saves enough money from her job, she's going to (OR she'll) buy a plane ticket.
3. . . . Vera goes home, she's going to buy presents for her family.
4. . . . Vera arrives at the airport, her father will be there to drive her home.
5. . . . Vera and her father get home, they'll have dinner.
6. Vera will give her family the presents . . . they finish dinner.
7. Vera's brother will wash the dishes . . . Vera's sister dries them.
8. The whole family is going to stay up talking . . . the clock strikes midnight.
9. . . . they go to bed, they'll all feel very tired.
10. Vera will fall asleep . . . her head hits the pillow.
11. . . . Vera wakes up the next morning, she's going to call her friends.
12. Vera will see her friends . . . she has breakfast.

EXERCISE 4

I have a lot of goals, but I need to get more

organized if I want to achieve them. So, tomorrow I'm

going to start working on them. College is my

number one goal. As soon as I ~~will~~ get up, I'm going to

download some online college catalogs. After I examine
                           'll OR *'m going to*
them carefully, I∧choose a few schools that interest
              'll OR *'m going to*
me and I∧try to set up some visits. Maybe I can even

get some interviews with some teachers at the schools.
             I visit
When ~~I'm going to visit~~ the schools, I'll also try to

speak to other students. That's always a good way to
                        see
find out about a place. After I ~~'m seeing~~ several schools,
'll OR *'m going to*
I∧decide which ones to apply to. When I get accepted,

I'll make the best choice. While I'm in school, I'll study
                  'll OR *'m going to*
hard and in four years I∧have my degree!

EXERCISE 5

Answers will vary.

PART 3 PRESENT PERFECT
UNIT 8 Present Perfect: *Since* and *For*

EXERCISE 1

2. broken
3. come
4. fallen
5. gone
6. had
7. lost

8. played
9. watched
10. won

EXERCISE 2

2. since
3. since
4. for
5. Since
6. For
7. for
8. since

EXERCISE 3

2. for
3. Since
4. has reached
5. Since
6. has gone on
7. has played
8. Since
9. has continued
10. has earned
11. For
12. has been
13. has been
14. since
15. has continued
16. since
17. Since
18. has broken
19. has . . . won
20. since
21. For
22. has had
23. has stopped
24. Since
25. 've dreamed
26. since
27. has not competed

EXERCISE 4

2. **A:** How long has she had a record-breaking career?
   B: She has had a record-breaking career since she was ten OR since she became the youngest player to qualify for the USGA amateur championship.
3. **A:** How long has she been a professional golfer?
   B: (She has been a professional golfer) since she was sixteen OR for _____ years.
4. **A:** Has she had any endorsement contracts?
   B: Yes, she has. (She has had endorsement contracts since she turned pro OR since she was sixteen.)
5. **A:** How long has Juan Martín del Potro been a tennis player?
   B: (He has been a tennis player) since he was seven OR for _____ years.
6. **A:** How much money has he won since he turned pro?
   B: He has won millions of dollars (since he turned pro).
7. **A:** What kind of problems has he had for years?
   B: He has had a lot of physical problems (for years).
8. **A:** Has he won any titles since 2008?
   B: Yes, he has. (He won the U.S. Open.)

EXERCISE 5

3. Min Ho has won three awards
4. Marilyn has entered two competitions
5. Victor and Marilyn haven't seen each other since 2015.
6. Karl has been a tennis player since 2014.
7. Karl has lost three tournaments
8. Andreas hasn't been to (OR gone to) a tennis match

EXERCISE 6

What a great game! Marissa has been my favorite
for
~~since~~ years!

I heard that Taylor got $350,000 for winning
 has he made
yesterday's tournament. How much money ~~does he make~~ since he turned pro? Does anyone know?

Do you think Lee can support himself playing golf?
 won
He hasn't ~~win~~ a major tournament for two years. That's a long time!
 hasn't won
Karla ~~didn't win~~ a game since last year. I really feel bad for her.

Walter has stopped playing twice since January because of injuries. That's really too bad.

I haven't had the opportunity to attend a
 for
competition ~~since~~ three years. This one is awesome!

I used to think golf was boring. Not anymore. I
haven't enjoyed
~~don't enjoy~~ a sports event so much for years!
 improved
I think Pedro's game has ~~improve~~ dramatically since he won the last tournament.
 has
Antonio's positive attitude ~~have~~ helped him improve his game since he lost the match last month. I consider him a role model.

EXERCISE 7

Answers will vary.

UNIT 9 Present Perfect: *Already, Yet,* and *Still*

EXERCISE 1

2. become
3. chosen
4. cleaned
5. danced
6. drunk
7. fought
8. found
9. gotten
10. given
11. held
12. kept
13. known
14. looked
15. planned
16. sung
17. smiled
18. thrown

EXERCISE 2

4. 've
5. already
6. looked
7. still
8. haven't found
9. 've
10. already
11. seen
12. haven't gone OR haven't been
13. yet
14. have
15. already
16. wasted
17. Have
18. decided
19. yet
20. haven't made up
21. yet

EXERCISE 3

3. Has she bought two bookcases yet? Yes, she's already bought two bookcases.
4. Has she thrown away old magazines yet? No, she hasn't thrown away old magazines yet. OR No, she hasn't yet thrown away old magazines. OR No, she still hasn't thrown away old magazines.
5. Has she found a professional painter yet? No, she hasn't found a professional painter yet. OR No, she hasn't yet found a professional painter. OR No, she still hasn't found a professional painter.
6. Has she collected boxes for packing yet? Yes, she's already collected boxes for packing.
7. Has she bought a new couch yet? No, she hasn't bought a new couch yet. OR No, she hasn't yet bought a new couch. OR No, she still hasn't bought a new couch.
8. Has she given away the old couch yet? Yes, she's already given away the old couch.
9. Has she cleaned the refrigerator and stove yet? No, she hasn't cleaned the refrigerator and stove yet. OR No, she hasn't yet cleaned the refrigerator and stove. OR No, she still hasn't cleaned the refrigerator and stove.
10. Has she made a list of cleaning supplies yet? Yes, she's already made a list of cleaning supplies.
11. Has she gotten a change-of-address form from the post office yet? Yes, she's already gotten a change-of-address form from the post office.
12. Has she invited the neighbors over for a good-bye party yet? No, she hasn't invited the neighbors over for a good-bye party yet. OR No, she hasn't yet invited the neighbors over for a good-bye party. OR No, she still hasn't invited the neighbors over for a good-bye party.

EXERCISE 4

I'm writing to you from our new apartment! It took

us a long time to find, but finally, with some

professional advice, we were successful. We've already

been
~~be~~ here two weeks, and we feel very much at home.

But there's still a lot to do. Believe it or not, we haven't

yet*
unpacked all the boxes ~~still~~! We took most of our old

furniture, so we don't need to get too much new stuff.

We had to buy a new couch for the living room, but

yet
they haven't delivered it ~~already~~.

met
We've already ~~meet~~ some of our new neighbors.

has
They seem very nice. One of them ~~have~~ already invited

us over for coffee.

Have
~~Had~~ you made vacation plans yet? As soon as we

get the couch (it's a sleeper), we'd love for you to visit.

We've already planned
~~Already we've planned~~ places to take you when you

come, but let us know if there are specific things you'd

like to do or see.

* OR . . . *still haven't unpacked* . . .

EXERCISE 5

Answers will vary.

UNIT 10 Present Perfect: Indefinite Past

EXERCISE 1

2. decided
3. flown
4. gone
5. heard
6. kept
7. made
8. ridden
9. seen
10. swum
11. traveled
12. worked

EXERCISE 2

2. 've ridden
3. 've heard
4. 've seen
5. 's flown
6. 've swum
7. has decided
8. 's worked

EXERCISE 3

2. have appeared
3. have . . . loved
4. have not stopped
5. has researched
6. (has) written
7. have . . . received
8. has described
9. has published

10. has created
11. have not become
12. have increased
13. has continued
14. has . . . encouraged
15. have not read

EXERCISE 4

2. How many times have you visited . . . I've visited Europe more than 10 times.
3. Have you ever been . . . Yes, I've recently been on an African safari.
4. Have you ever been . . . Yes, I've been to Costa Rica.
5. How often have you been . . . I've been there once.
6. Have you ever traveled . . . No, I've never traveled in China.
7. Have you ever gone up . . . No, I've never gone up in a hot-air balloon.
8. Have you ever swum . . . I've swum with dolphins many times (OR six or more times).
9. Have you ever taken . . . No, I've never taken a group tour.

EXERCISE 5

ever been
Q: Have you ~~been ever~~ to Barcelona? I'm planning a trip

there this summer and would love some tips.

A: I've never been there, but you can find a lot of useful

information on websites such as tripadvisor.com.

returned
Q: I~~'ve returned~~ last week from a safari in Africa. It was

awesome, and I'm really interested in sharing photos

with other travelers. Any ideas?

A: Yes! We've recently formed an online discussion

group on safaris and we post photos there. Contact

me at travcal@oal.com for more information.

Q: I'm trying to choose a hotel for my trip to Toronto.

stayed
Has anyone you know ever ~~stays~~ at the Victoria?

stayed there several times
A: I've ~~several times stayed there~~ myself. It's convenient

and affordable. I think you'd like it.

Q: I'm going to be traveling alone in the south of

France. What's the best form of transportation for

getting around? I can't afford to rent a car.

taken
A: I've always ~~took~~ local buses. They're comfortable

and you get to see a lot of the countryside.

Q: Have you read the results of *Travel Today's* annual

have
survey? It seems like a lot of people ~~has~~ decided to

take vacations closer to home. And many people

chosen
have ~~choose~~ not to go away at all this summer.
    just booked
A: Not me! I've ~~booked just~~ a vacation to Australia. I've
been
never ~~was~~ to that part of the world, and I can't wait

to go!

EXERCISE 6

Answers will vary.

UNIT 11 Present Perfect and Simple Past

EXERCISE 1

2. become
3. begun
4. buy
5. decided, decided
6. felt
7. get, got
8. gave, given
9. went, gone
10. had
11. live, lived
12. make
13. met, met
14. moved, moved
15. paid, paid
16. read, read
17. risen
18. see, saw
19. started, started
20. take, took

EXERCISE 2

3. Tom has gone OR has been
4. Tom got
5. Tom has made
6. Tom met
7. Tom has been
8. Tom looked
9. Tom bought
10. Tom has paid
11. Tom has read
12. Tom has managed
13. Tom has given
14. Tom felt

EXERCISE 3

2. got
3. 've been
4. did . . . have
5. became
6. had
7. were
8. did . . . last
9. divorced
10. Did . . . have
11. didn't
12. 've managed
13. saw
14. have become
15. Has . . . remarried
16. hasn't
17. did . . . fail
18. got
19. didn't know
20. did . . . meet
21. were
22. did . . . move
23. 've lived

EXERCISE 4

2. began
3. got
4. had
5. was
6. has risen
7. occurred
8. has created
9. started
10. had
11. were
12. has . . . increased
13. stayed
14. got
15. has changed
16. has reached

EXERCISE 5

          met
Last month, I ~~have met~~ the most wonderful guy. His

name is Roger, and he's a student in my night class. He
's lived
~~lived~~ here since 2014. Before that, he lived in Detroit,
                                      was
too—so we have a lot in common. Roger ~~has been~~

married for five years, but got divorced last April.
              have managed
Roger and I ~~managed~~ to spend a lot of time together

in spite of our busy schedules. Last week, I saw him
                     we've
every night, and this week ~~we~~ already gotten together

three times after class. I find that I miss him when we're

apart!
                    saw   *Have you seen*
Monday night we ~~have seen~~ a great movie. ~~Did you~~
~~see~~ The Purple Room? It's playing in all the theaters now.

We've decided to take a trip back to Detroit in the

summer. Maybe we can get together. It would be great

to see you again. Please let me know if you'll be there.
                                 took
P.S. Here's a photo of Roger that I ~~'ve taken~~ a few

weeks ago.

EXERCISE 6

Answers will vary.

UNIT 12 Present Perfect Progressive and Present

EXERCISE 1

2. She's been writing articles about global warming
   since last month OR for a month.
3. Amanda and Pete haven't been living in New York
   since a few years ago OR for a few years.
4. They've been living in Toronto since 2013 OR for
   _____ years.
5. They've been driving a fuel-efficient car since last
   year OR for a year.
6. Pete hasn't been working since last year OR for a
   year.

7. Pete and Amanda have been thinking of traveling to Africa since last year OR for a year.

8. Amanda has been reading a lot about Africa for a few months OR since a few months ago.

9. Pete has been studying zoology since last month OR for a month OR since he went back to school (last month).

10. Amanda and Pete have been looking for a new apartment since a month ago OR for a month.

EXERCISE 2

2. has written
3. has won
4. has been
5. has received
6. has been working
7. has been teaching
8. has been taking
9. has stopped
10. has . . . been organizing
11. has designed
12. (has) developed
13. have been watching
14. has not been teaching
15. has not stopped
16. has been traveling
17. (has been) giving
18. has gone

EXERCISE 3

2. They've been eating meat-free meals one day a week.
3. They've been using pesticides.
4. They've been choosing (OR They've chosen) energy-efficient appliances.
5. They've been reducing (OR They've reduced) home heating and electricity use.
6. They haven't been recycling paper, cans, and bottles.
7. They've bought a fuel-efficient car.
8. They haven't been walking, biking, carpooling, or taking public transportation.
9. They haven't chosen a home close to work or school.
10. They haven't taken a vacation close to home.

EXERCISE 4

2. Has he won any awards?
   Yes. He's won many awards.
3. How long has he been retired?
   He's been retired since 2001 (OR for _____ years).
4. How many honorary degrees has he received?
   He's received more than 20.
5. How long has his foundation existed?
   It's existed since 1990 (OR for _____ years).
6. What has the Foundation been teaching young people?
   It's been teaching them about the importance of a healthy environment.
7. What activity has Suzuki stopped?
   He's stopped going on vacations that require air travel.
8. Has he developed a lot of TV shows?
   Yes. He's developed many TV shows.

9. How long have people been watching *The Nature of Things?*
   They've been watching it since 1960 (OR for _____ years).
10. What has Suzuki been doing to spread his message?
   He's been traveling and giving speeches.

EXERCISE 5

It's the second week of the fall semester. I've ~~taken~~ *been taking* a course on environmental issues with Professor McCarthy. He's an expert on the subject of global warming, and he's already ~~been writing~~ *written* two books on the topic. I think one of them has even ~~been winning~~ *won* an award.

For the past two weeks, we've ∧ *been* studying pollution and how the Earth's temperature ~~have~~ *has* been getting warmer. As part of the course, we've been reading a lot of books on the environment. For example, I've just ~~been finishing~~ *finished* a book called *The Sacred Balance: Rediscovering Our Place in Nature* by David Suzuki. He's a well-known Canadian scientist and environmentalist. It was fascinating. Since then, I've also ~~read~~ *been reading* his autobiography. I've only ~~been reading~~ *read* about 50 pages of the book so far, but it seems interesting, too. I'm really learning a lot in this course, and I've ~~been~~ started to change some of the things I do in order to help protect the planet.

EXERCISE 6

Answers will vary.

PART 4 MODALS AND SIMILAR EXPRESSIONS
UNIT 13 Ability and Possibility: *Can, Could, Be able to*

EXERCISE 1

3. can read an English newspaper . . . could (read one)
4. couldn't read an English novel . . . can't (read one)
5. can speak on the phone . . . couldn't (speak on the phone)
6. couldn't speak with a group of people . . . can (speak with a group of people)
7. could write an email . . . can (write one)

8. Before the course, he couldn't write a business letter, and he still can't (write one).

9. Now he can order a meal in English, and he could (order a meal in English) before, too.

10. Now he can go shopping, and he could (go shopping) before, too.

11. can . . . could

EXERCISE 2

2. A: What languages can you speak?

3. A: Could you speak Spanish when you were a child?
   B: No, I couldn't.

4. A: Could you speak French?
   B: Yes, I could.

5. A: Before you came here, could you understand spoken English?
   B: No, I couldn't.

6. A: Can you understand song lyrics?
   B: Yes, I can.

7. A: Before this course, could you write a business letter in English?
   B: No, I couldn't.

8. A: Could you drive a car before you came here?
   B: No, I couldn't.

9. A: Can you drive a car now?
   B: No, I can't.

10. A: Can you swim?
    B: Yes, I can.

11. A: Could you surf before you came here?
    B: No, I couldn't.

12. A: What can you do now that you couldn't do before?
    B: can do . . . couldn't do

EXERCISE 3

2. can damage
3. can recover
4. can't survive
5. can lose
6. can listen
7. can . . . do
8. can understand
9. can't leave
10. can't be

EXERCISE 4

2. are able to interpret
3. are not able to distinguish
4. are not able to understand
5. are able to hear
6. are able to get back
7. are able to read
8. is not able to recognize
9. is not able to work
10. are able to communicate

EXERCISE 5

3. How will . . . be able to see
4. Will . . . be able to hear
5. No, you won't.

6. How will . . . be able to solve
7. Will . . . be able to enjoy
8. Yes, you will.

EXERCISE 6

2. could read
3. couldn't accept
4. was able to accept
5. could see
6. will . . . be able to do
7. can do
8. can do
9. can speak
10. was able to achieve
11. will be able to get
12. can read
13. will be able to enjoy
14. can change
15. can do

EXERCISE 7

Before I came to this country, I ~~can't~~ *couldn't* do many things in English. For example, I couldn't follow a conversation if many people were talking at the same time. I always got confused. I remember a party I went to. Everyone was speaking English, and I wasn't able *to* ^understand a word! I felt so uncomfortable. Finally, my aunt came to pick me up, and I ~~could~~ *was able to* leave the party.

Today, I can ⊠ understand much better. I am taking classes at the adult center. My teacher is very good. She can ~~explains~~ *explain* things well, and she always gives us the chance to talk a lot in class. When I finish this class in May, I ~~can~~ *will be able to* speak and understand a lot better.

Speaking English well is very important to me. I practice a lot at home, too. When I first came to this country, I ~~can't~~ *couldn't* OR *wasn't able to* understand very much TV, but now I can ⊠ understand much better. In fact, I can do a lot now, and I think in a few more months I ~~can~~ *'ll be able to* do even more.

EXERCISE 8

Answers will vary.

UNIT 14 Permission: *Can, Could, May, Do you mind if*

EXERCISE 1

2. c
3. b
4. h
5. f
6. a
7. e
8. g

EXERCISE 2

2. we (please) review Unit 6? OR we review Unit 6, please?
3. I (please) borrow your pen? OR I borrow your pen, please?
4. I look at your (class) notes?
5. I come late to the next class?
6. my roommate (please) come to the next class with me? OR my roommate come to the next class with me, please?
7. I (please) ask a question? OR I ask a question, please?
8. we (please) use a dictionary? OR we use a dictionary, please?
9. we (please) leave five minutes early? OR we leave five minutes early, please?
10. my sister goes on the class trip with the rest of the class?

EXERCISE 3

2. can bring
3. can bring
4. can't OR cannot drink
5. can pay
6. can pay
7. may not pay
8. may not purchase
9. can't OR cannot get
10. may swim

EXERCISE 4

I've been sick for the past two days. That's why I missed the last test. I'm really annoyed. I studied a lot for it and was really well prepared. May I ~~taking~~ *take* a make-up exam?

I know you never miss class, Tim, so I assumed that's what happened. I hope you're feeling better. Yes, you can take a make-up exam if you bring a doctor's note.

If I can take the exam, may I use a calculator during the test?

No, you ~~mayn't~~ *may not*! It's against the guidelines we established at the beginning of the semester. Remember?

Could my roommate ~~comes~~ *come* to class and take notes for me on Thursday?

Yes, he ~~could~~ *can*. I hope you can read his handwriting!

Do you mind ~~when~~ *if* he records Allison's presentation for me? I don't want to miss it.

Not at all. It's fine for him to record the presentation.

One last thing—I know I missed some handouts.

May I ~~have please~~ *please have* copies of them?

Sure. I'll give them to your roommate on Thursday.

Thanks a lot.

EXERCISE 5

Answers will vary.

UNIT 15 Requests: *Can, Could, Will, Would, Would you mind*

EXERCISE 1

2. a
3. h
4. g
5. j
6. c
7. b
8. i
9. f
10. e

"Yes" responses: b, c, e, f, g, j
"No" responses: d, h, i
Negative word meaning "OK, I'll do it": j

EXERCISE 2

2. opening the window
3. buy some stamps
4. pick up a sandwich
5. staying late tonight
6. keep the noise down
7. come to my office
8. get Frank's phone number
9. explaining this note to me
10. lend me $5.00

EXERCISE 3

2. Would you mind working on Saturday?
3. Will you please help me? OR Will you help me, please?
4. Would you please text me your decision? OR Would you text me your decision, please?
5. Could you please drive me home? OR Could you drive me home, please?

EXERCISE 4

Note 3. Will you return please the stapler? → Will you please return the stapler? OR Will you return the stapler, please?
Note 5. Would you mind deliver → Would you mind delivering
Note 6. Could you please remember to lock the door. → Could you please remember to lock the door?
Note 7. Would you please to call Ms. Rivera before the end of the day? → Would you please call Ms. Rivera before the end of the day? OR Would you call Ms. Rivera before the end of the day, please?

Note 8. Also, would you mind to email Lisa Barker a
copy? → Also, would you mind emailing Lisa Barker
a copy?

EXERCISE 5

Answers will vary.

UNIT 16 Advice: *Should, Ought to, Had better*

EXERCISE 1

2. You shouldn't shout into the phone.
3. You should speak in a quiet, normal voice.
4. You should leave the room to make a phone call.
5. You shouldn't discuss private issues in public places. You should protect your own and other people's privacy.
6. You shouldn't stand too close to other people when you are talking on the phone.
7. You should pay attention to other people on the street when you are walking and talking.
8. You shouldn't use a cell phone when you are driving. OR You should never use a cell phone when you are driving.

EXERCISE 2

2. should call
3. 'd better not forget
4. ought to see . . . 'd better buy . . . should get
5. should try
6. ought to think . . . should look into
7. shouldn't talk . . . should be
8. 'd better not call
9. ought to have
10. should get
11. ought to have
12. shouldn't talk
13. 'd better hang up

EXERCISE 3

3. What should I wear?
4. Should I bring a gift?
5. No, you shouldn't.
6. Should I bring something to eat or drink?
7. You should bring something to drink.
8. When should I respond?
9. You should respond by May 15.
10. Should I call Aunt Rosa?
11. No, you shouldn't.
12. Who should I call?
13. You should call Amy (and leave a message at 555–3234).

EXERCISE 4

1. You're at a party and you can't remember someone's
   name. What ~~you should~~ *should you* do?
   a. You should ~~no~~ *not* ask the person's name.

b. ~~You better~~ *You'd better* avoid the person or leave immediately!
c. You ought ∧ *to* just ask.

2. You don't know anyone at the party, and your host doesn't introduce you to the other guests. ~~Had you better~~ *Should you* introduce yourself?
   a. Yes, you should. You should say, "Hi. My name's
      _____."
   b. No, you ~~should~~ *shouldn't*. You'd better tell the host to introduce you.

3. Your cell phone rings during the party. ~~You should~~ *Should you* answer it?
   a. Just let it ring. You ~~had not better~~ *'d better not* answer it.
   b. You should answer it, but just have a short conversation.
   c. You really ought to leave the room and speak to the person in private.

4. You had a very nice time at the party. How ~~you should~~ *should you* thank your host?
   a. You should just say "thank you" when you leave.
   b. You should send a "thank-you" email the next day.
   c. You ~~oughta~~ *ought to* write a long "thank-you" letter and send a gift, too.

5. Everyone brought gifts to the party. You didn't.
   a. You'd better ̶X̶ apologize right away.
   b. You shouldn't say anything, but you ought to send a gift later.
   c. You should leave immediately and go buy a gift.

EXERCISE 5

Answers will vary.

PART 5 NOUNS, QUANTIFIERS, AND ARTICLES
UNIT 17 Nouns and Quantifiers

EXERCISE 1

A.

Tut's Tomb: An Egyptian <u>Time Capsule</u>
<u>Tutankhamun</u>, better known as <u>King Tut</u>, became <u>king</u>
of ancient <u>Egypt</u> when he was only nine <u>years</u> old.

He died before his nineteenth birthday around 1323 B.C.E., and was mostly forgotten. Thousands of years later, British archeologist Howard Carter searched for his tomb. In 1922, after searching for many years, he finally found it near the Nile River, across from the modern Egyptian city of Luxor. Inside he discovered thousands of items buried along with the young king. Among the many treasures were:

- furniture—including couches and chairs
- jewelry—including bracelets and necklaces
- clothing—including gloves, scarves, and shoes
- musical instruments
- chariots
- vases and jars
- pots made of clay (they probably once contained money)
- games and toys (Tut played with them as a child)
- food and wine
- gold

Tut's tomb is a time capsule. It gives us a picture of how Egyptian kings lived more than 3000 years ago, how they died, and what they expected to need in their lives after death.

Since his discovery, Tut has not been resting in peace. He and his treasures have traveled to exhibitions around the world, where millions of visitors have been able to view some of the wonders of his ancient civilization.

B.

Proper nouns: Tut, Tutankhamun, King Tut, Egypt, Howard Carter, Nile River, Luxor

Common count nouns: *Answers will vary. Some possibilities:* tomb, time capsule, years, birthday, archeologist, river, city, items, king, treasures, couches, chairs, bracelets, necklaces, gloves, scarves, shoes, instruments, chariots, vases, jars, pots, games, toys, child, picture, lives, discovery, exhibitions, world, visitors, wonders, civilization

Common non-count nouns: furniture, jewelry, clothing, clay, money, food, wine, gold, death, peace

EXERCISE 2

2. country lies
3. people live
4. Cairo has
5. Cotton is
6. Rice grows
7. tourists visit
8. Ramadan takes place
9. shops and restaurants close
10. weather is
11. clothing is
12. sunhats are OR a sunhat is

EXERCISE 3

2. many
3. several
4. a few
5. many
6. a lot of
7. much
8. many
9. much
10. some
11. a lot of
12. a few
13. some
14. a lot of
15. some
16. some
17. some
18. many
19. Many
20. many
21. a lot of

EXERCISE 4

I can't tell you how much we enjoyed our trip
to ~~egypt~~ *Egypt*. We just returned ~~few~~ *a few* days ago. What an
amazing country! There are so ~~much~~ *many* things to see and
do. My only complaint ~~are~~ *is* that we didn't have enough
time! But, we'll be back!

Hans Koch, Germany

We saw a lot of tombs and pyramids on our recent
trip, but the best were the three Giza pyramids. ~~It is~~ *They are*
huge! And, I was surprised to learn, they are located
right at the edge of the city of Cairo. Because of this,
there is a lot of traffic getting there (and back). There
were also a lot ∧ *of* tourists. The day we were there it was
very hot. If you go, you should know that there are
~~a few~~ *few* places to get anything to drink, so I REALLY
recommend that you bring ~~any~~ *some* water with you. Oh,
and if you want to see the inside of a pyramid, you
need a special ticket, and they only sell a ~~little~~ *few* tickets
each day. Get there early if you want one!

Vilma Ortiz, USA

The food ~~are~~ *is* great in Egypt! We went to some
wonderful ~~Restaurants~~ *restaurants*. We found out about one
place near our hotel that doesn't have ~~much~~ *many* tourists.
Mostly local people ~~eats~~ *eat* there and everyone was really
friendly. I particularly enjoyed the "meze" (a variety of
appetizers). You choose a ~~little~~ *few* different plates before
you order your main dish. Delicious!

Jim Cook, England

There are many beautiful ~~beach~~ *beaches* in Alexandria. A lot of them are private or connected to hotels, but there are also public ones, so be sure to bring a bathing suit if you visit that part of Egypt. The water ~~were~~ *was* warm— I felt like in a bathtub!

Aki Kato, Japan

EXERCISE 5

Answers will vary.

UNIT 18 Articles: Indefinite and Definite

EXERCISE 1

1. the, the	7. Ø, Ø, the, Ø
2. the	8. the, an, the
3. the	9. an, a
4. the, the	10. Ø, Ø
5. a, The, the	11. some, a, the, the
6. the	12. the, a, The

EXERCISE 2

2. a	8. a	14. the	19. an
3. the	9. –	15. the	20. –
4. A	10. The	16. the	21. a
5. a	11. –	17. the	22. –
6. –	12. a	18. the	23. the
7. –	13. The		

EXERCISE 3

2. a	9. the	16. the	22. the
3. a	10. The	17. the	23. The
4. the	11. the	18. The	24. the
5. the	12. a	19. a	25. the
6. the	13. the	20. the	26. –
7. the	14. the	21. the	27. the
8. the	15. an		

EXERCISE 4

A fox is ~~the~~ *a* member of the dog family. It looks like ~~the~~ *a* small, thin dog with ~~an~~ *a* bushy tail, a long nose, and pointed ears. You can find ~~the~~ foxes in most parts of ~~a~~ *the* world. ~~Animal~~ *The animal* moves very fast, and it is ~~the~~ *a* very good hunter. It eats mostly mice, but it also eats ~~the~~ birds, insects, rabbits, and fruit.

Unfortunately, ~~X~~ people hunt foxes for their beautiful fur. They also hunt them for another reason. The fox is ~~a~~ *an* intelligent, clever animal, and this makes it hard to catch. As a result, ~~the~~ hunters find it exciting to try to catch one. It is also because of its cleverness that a fox often appears in fables, such as ~~a~~ *the* fable we just read in class.

EXERCISE 5

Answers will vary.

PART 6 ADJECTIVES AND ADVERBS
UNIT 19 Adjectives and Adverbs

EXERCISE 1

3. fast	11. sudden
4. well	12. peacefully
5. dangerous	13. angrily
6. beautifully	14. convenient
7. hard	15. badly
8. safely	16. thoughtful
9. ideal	17. hungry
10. happy	18. extremely

EXERCISE 2

2. Good news travels fast
3. It has five large rooms
4. it's in a very large building
5. it's very sunny
6. We're really satisfied with it
7. It's not too bad
8. It seems quite pretty
9. he speaks very loudly
10. He doesn't hear well
11. Was it a hard decision
12. we had to decide quickly
13. I have to leave now
14. Good luck with your new apartment

EXERCISE 3

2. hard	16. empty
3. really	17. good
4. well	18. easily
5. nice	19. near
6. extremely	20. frequently
7. comfortable	21. nice
8. cold	22. convenient
9. pretty	23. wonderful
10. friendly	24. completely
11. safe	25. new
12. really	26. really
13. important	27. happy
14. late	28. happy
15. completely	

EXERCISE 4

2. disturbed
3. entertaining
4. disgusted
5. inspiring
6. paralyzed
7. moving
8. moved
9. frightening
10. disturbed
11. touching
12. astonishing
13. frightening
14. bored
15. disappointed
16. touching
17. exciting
18. entertaining
19. bored

EXERCISE 5

2. tall handsome Italian actor
3. large new TV
4. delicious fresh mushroom pizza
5. comfortable black leather sofa
6. nice small student apartment
7. quiet residential neighborhood
8. enjoyable, relaxing evening
9. small comfortable, affordable apartment (OR small affordable, comfortable apartment)

EXERCISE 6

Charming
~~Charmingly~~, one-bedroom apartment in a ~~residential~~ *peaceful residential*
Conveniently
~~peaceful~~ neighborhood. ~~Convenient~~ located near

shopping, transportation, entertainment, and more.

- affordable rent
- all-new appliances
  beautiful antique French
- ~~French antique beautiful~~ desk
- friendly neighbors
  safe
- clean and ~~safely~~ neighborhood
  close
- ~~closely~~ to park
- quiet building

This great apartment is ideal for students, and
available immediately
it's ~~immediate available~~. Call 444–HOME for an
disappointed
appointment. You won't be ~~disappointing~~! But act
fast   *amazing apartment*
~~fastly~~! This ~~apartment amazing~~ won't last long.

EXERCISE 7

Answers will vary.

UNIT 20 Adjectives: Comparisons with *As . . . as* and *Than*

EXERCISE 1

2. worse
3. bigger
4. more careful
5. cheaper
6. more comfortable
7. more crowded
8. more delicious
9. earlier
10. more expensive
11. farther (OR further)
12. fresher
13. better
14. hotter
15. noisier
16. more relaxed
17. more terrible
18. more traditional
19. more varied
20. wetter

EXERCISE 2

2. not as large as
3. just as big as
4. just as expensive as
5. not as varied as
6. not as long as
7. not as convenient as
8. not as late as
9. not as nice as
10. just as good as
11. just as clean as
12. not as good as

EXERCISE 3

2. earlier
3. more comfortable
4. healthier than
5. more interesting than, better than, fresher
6. taller than
7. worse, quieter than (OR more quiet than), more relaxed
8. later than
9. faster
10. easier

EXERCISE 4

2. Y . . . cheaper than . . . X
3. Y . . . larger than . . . X
4. X . . . smaller than . . . Y
5. Y . . . heavier than . . . X
6. X . . . lighter than . . . Y
7. X . . . more efficient than . . . Y
8. Y . . . more effective than . . . X
9. Y . . . faster than . . . X
10. X . . . slower than . . . Y
11. X . . . noisier than . . . Y
12. Y . . . quieter (OR more quiet) than . . . X
13. Y . . . better than . . . X
14. X . . . worse than . . . Y

EXERCISE 5

2. cheaper and cheaper (OR less and less expensive)
3. better and better
4. bigger and bigger
5. more and more varied
6. more and more popular

7. less and less healthy

8. heavier and heavier

EXERCISE 6

2. The fresher the ingredients, the better the food.

3. The more popular the restaurant, the longer the lines.

4. The more enjoyable the meal, the more satisfied the customers.

5. The bigger the selection, the happier the customers.

6. The later in the day, the more tired the servers (get).

7. The more crowded the restaurant, the slower the service.

8. The better the service, the higher the tip.

EXERCISE 7

I just got home from the Pizza Palace. Wow! The pizza there just keeps getting ~~good~~ *better* and better. And, of course, the better the food, the ~~more long~~ *longer* the lines, and the ~~crowdeder~~ *more crowded* the restaurant! But I don't really mind. It's totally worth it. Tonight, Ana and I shared a pizza with spinach, mushrooms, and ~~fresher~~ *fresh* tomatoes. It was much more interesting ~~as~~ *than* a traditional pizza with just tomato sauce and cheese. It's also healthier ~~than~~. And the ingredients were as fresh ~~than~~ *as* you can find anywhere in the city. (Although I usually think the pizza at Joe's Pizzeria is fresher.) It was so large that we couldn't finish it, so I brought the rest home. Actually, I'm getting hungry again just thinking about it. I think I'll pop a slice into the microwave and warm it up. It will probably taste almost as ~~better~~ *good* as it tasted at the Pizza Palace!

EXERCISE 8

Answers will vary.

UNIT 21 Adjectives: Superlatives

EXERCISE 1

2. the worst

3. the biggest

4. the cutest

5. the most dynamic

6. the most expensive

7. the farthest (OR the furthest)

8. the funniest

9. the best

10. the happiest (OR the most happy)

11. the hottest

12. the most important

13. the most intelligent

14. the most interesting

15. the lowest

16. the nicest

17. the noisiest (OR the most noisy)

18. the most practical

19. the warmest

20. the most wonderful

EXERCISE 2

2. Mexico City . . . the newest

3. New York City . . . the longest

4. Toronto . . . the shortest

5. The busiest . . . New York City

6. Toronto . . . the lowest

7. New York City . . . the most expensive (OR Mexico City . . . the least expensive)

8. the cheapest . . . Mexico City

EXERCISE 3

2. the newest

3. the most beautiful

4. the easiest

5. the biggest

6. the least comfortable

7. the fastest

8. the coolest

9. the hottest

10. the most convenient

11. the most interesting

12. the least dangerous

13. the most historic

14. the most crowded

15. The most efficient

16. the most dangerous

17. the least expensive

18. the quietest (OR the most quiet)

EXERCISE 4

Greetings from Mexico City! With its mixture of the old and the new, this is one of the ~~interestingest~~ *most interesting* cities I've ever visited. The people are among the ~~friendlier~~ *friendliest* OR *most friendly* in the world, and they have been very patient with my attempts to speak their language. Spanish is definitely one of ~~a~~ *the* most beautiful languages, and I really want to take lessons when I get home.

This has been the ~~most hot~~ *hottest* summer in years, and I'm looking forward to going to the beach next week.

The air pollution is also the ~~baddest~~ *worst* I've experienced, so

I'll be glad to be out of the city.

By the way, we definitely did not need to rent a car.
The ~~most fast~~ *fastest* and ~~convenientest~~ *most convenient* way to get around

is by subway.

EXERCISE 5

Answers will vary.

UNIT 22 Adverbs: As . . . as, Comparatives, Superlatives

EXERCISE 1

2. worse, the worst
3. more beautifully, the most beautifully
4. more carefully, the most carefully
5. more consistently, the most consistently
6. more dangerously, the most dangerously
7. earlier, the earliest
8. more effectively, the most effectively
9. farther (OR further), the farthest (OR the furthest)
10. faster, the fastest
11. more frequently, the most frequently
12. harder, the hardest
13. more intensely, the most intensely
14. less, the least
15. longer, the longest
16. more, the most
17. more quickly, the most quickly
18. more slowly, the most slowly
19. sooner, the soonest
20. better, the best

EXERCISE 2

2. ran as fast as
3. jumped as high as
4. didn't jump as high as
5. didn't throw the discus as far as
6. threw the discus as far as
7. didn't do as well as
8. didn't compete as successfully as

EXERCISE 3

2. harder than
3. more slowly than OR slower than
4. faster
5. more consistently
6. more aggressively than
7. worse than
8. better
9. more effectively

10. more intensely
11. (more) frequently
Winning Team: Jamil, Randy, Carlos
Losing Team: Alex, Rick, Larry, Elvin

EXERCISE 4

2. E . . . the most slowly (OR the slowest), more slowly than (OR slower than)
3. higher than . . . B
4. E . . . the highest
5. farther than . . . E
6. E . . . the farthest
7. E . . . the best
8. E . . . the worst . . . better than

EXERCISE 5

2. She's running more and more frequently.
3. He's throwing the ball farther and farther.
4. She's shooting more and more accurately.
5. He's jumping higher and higher.
6. He's running more and more slowly OR slower and slower.
7. They're skating (OR dancing) more and more gracefully.
8. They're practicing longer and longer.
9. He's driving more and more dangerously.
10. They're feeling worse and worse.

EXERCISE 6

Tuesday, June 11

I just completed my run. I'm running much longer ~~that~~ *than*

before.

Wednesday, June 12

Today I ran for 30 minutes without getting out of
breath. I'm glad I decided to run ~~more slow~~ *more slowly OR slower*. The more
slowly I run, the ~~farthest~~ *farther* I can go. I'm really seeing

progress.

Thursday, June 13

Because I'm enjoying it, I run more and more ~~frequent~~ *frequently*.

And the more often I do it, the longer and farther I can

go. I really believe that running helps me feel better
more ~~quick~~ *quickly* than other forms of exercise. I'm even

sleeping better than before!

Friday, June 14

I'm thinking about running in the next marathon. I

as fast as OR *faster than*
may not run ~~as fast than~~ younger runners, but I think I
longer
can run ~~long~~ and farther. We'll see!

EXERCISE 7

Answers will vary.

EXERCISE 1

2. going
3. meeting
4. Sitting
5. running
6. lifting
7. doing
8. taking
9. Exercising
10. wasting

EXERCISE 2

2. Dancing
3. lifting weights
4. walking (OR playing tennis) . . . playing tennis (OR walking)
5. swimming
6. lifting weights
7. walking (OR riding a bike) . . . riding a bike (OR walking)
8. Doing sit-ups
9. swimming
10. lifting weights (OR doing sit-ups) . . . doing sit-ups (OR lifting weights)
11. running
12. playing tennis
13. Riding a bike
14. lifting weights

EXERCISE 3

2. dislikes doing OR doesn't enjoy doing
3. enjoys dancing
4. mind teaching
5. kept practicing
6. denied (OR denies) stepping OR didn't admit (OR doesn't admit) stepping
7. considering taking
8. regrets not beginning
9. suggests going OR suggested going
10. admits feeling OR admitted feeling
11. banned smoking OR doesn't permit smoking
12. permits smoking

EXERCISE 4

2. to having
3. in quitting
4. about passing
5. on staying, finishing
6. of staying, of getting

7. in having
8. of permitting, to smoking

EXERCISE 5

banning
I'm in favor of ~~ban~~ smoking in all public places.
smoking
I think ~~to smoke~~ should be illegal in parks and at beaches.
of
I approve ~~to~~ having free programs that help people quit
smoking
~~to smoke~~.
Advertising
~~To advertise~~ cigarettes in newspapers and magazines is
alright.
is
Smoking cigarettes ~~are~~ a private decision, and the
government should not make laws against it.
lighting
If people enjoy ~~to light~~ up cigarettes, that is their right.

EXERCISE 6

Answers will vary.

EXERCISE 1

2. want to see
3. refuses to go
4. threatened to end
5. hesitate (OR am hesitating) to take
6. seems to be
7. attempted to create
8. intend to stay
9. needs to speak
10. will agree to go

EXERCISE 2

2. to do the dishes.
   him to do the dishes.
3. her to buy some milk.
   to buy some milk.
4. him to drive her to her aunt's.
   to drive her to her aunt's.
5. him to have dinner at her place Friday night.
   to have dinner at her place Friday night.
6. him to give her his answer tomorrow.
   to give her his answer tomorrow.
7. to cut his hair.
   her to cut his hair.
8. him to be home at 7:00.
   to get home at 8:00.
9. her to call him before she left the office.
   to call him before she left the office.
10. to see a movie Friday night.
    her to pick one.

11. to ask his boss for a raise.
    him to do it.
12. to get some more stamps.
    to stop at the post office on the way home.

EXERCISE 3

      Ana answered my letter. I didn't expect ~~hearing~~ *to hear* back

from her so soon! She agrees that seeing a counselor is

a good idea for John and me, but she advised ~~we~~ *us* to go

to counseling separately at first. That idea never even

occurred to me, but I think that it's a really excellent

suggestion. I don't know if John will agree ~~going~~ *to go*, but

I'm definitely going to ask him to think about it when I

see him on Saturday. I attempted to introduce the topic

last night, but he pretended ~~to not~~ *not to* hear me. (He's been

doing that a lot lately. He seems to think if he ignores a

question, I'll just forget about it!) I won't give up,

though. I'm going to try to persuade ~~he~~ *him* to go. I have

no idea how to find a counselor, so if he agrees to

go, I may ask Ana ∧ *to* recommend someone in our area.

Obviously, I want ~~finding~~ *to find* someone really good.

      I still believe in us as a couple. Our relationship

deserves to have a chance, and I'm prepared ∧ *to* give it

one. But I want John ~~feels~~ *to feel* the same way. After all, it

takes more than one person to make a relationship. I

really need to know that he's 100 percent committed to

the relationship. I can be patient, but I can't afford

~~waiting~~ *to wait* forever.

EXERCISE 4

Answers will vary.

UNIT 25 More Uses of Infinitives

EXERCISE 1

2. Nate can use his cell phone or smartphone to take pictures.
3. Nate can use his smartphone to search online.
4. Nate can use his smartphone to send emails.
5. Nate can use his cell phone or smartphone to connect to the Internet.
6. Nate can use his smartphone to create a "To Do" list.

7. Nate can use his cell phone or smartphone to store addresses.
8. Nate can use his smartphone to play music.
9. Nate can use his smartphone to translate words.

EXERCISE 2

3. He uses most of his salary (in order) to pay his college tuition.
4. He really wants a smartwatch (in order) to read text messages while jogging.
5. He's going to wait for a sale in order not to pay the full price.
6. A lot of people came into the store today (in order) to look at the new multipurpose devices.
7. They like talking to Ed (in order) to get information about the devices.
8. Someone bought a GPS in order not to get lost.
9. Another person bought a robot vacuum (in order) to do less housework.
10. She used her credit card in order not to pay right away.
11. Ed showed her how to use the robot vacuum (in order) to clean a large room.
12. She'll use it in her apartment (in order) to save time.

EXERCISE 3

2. to have
3. to pay
4. to eat
5. to leave
6. to take
7. to find

EXERCISE 4

2. good enough for me to do
3. too late to go
4. fast enough to leave
5. too tired to stay
6. too late to call
7. clearly enough for me to understand
8. hot enough to need
9. too hot for me to drink
10. easy enough for him to program

EXERCISE 5

Andrea (4:45 p.m.): Did you call Sara ~~for reminding~~ *to remind*

her about dinner tomorrow night?

Me (4:50 p.m.): It's ~~to~~ *too* early to call now. Don't worry.

I set my alarm in order ~~no~~ *not* to forget.

Andrea (5:30 p.m.): Will you be home ~~enough early~~ *early enough* to

help me with dinner?

Me (5:45 p.m.): Not sure. I have to stop at the

hardware store ~~too~~ *to* buy some more paint for the

kitchen.

Andrea (6:00 p.m.): Don't we still have paint?

Me (6:05 p.m.): Yes. But I want to make sure we have

enough paint to ~~finishes~~ *finish* the job. It'll be a major

improvement.

Andrea (6:10 p.m.): OK. Would it be too hard ~~to~~ *for* you

to make another stop on the way home? I need some

butter and eggs ~~for baking~~ *to bake* the cake for tomorrow

night. ☺

Me (6:15 p.m.): No problem. See you soon. XOXOX

EXERCISE 6
Answers will vary.

UNIT 26 Gerunds and Infinitives

EXERCISE 1

2. living
3. Flying
4. to get
5. flying
6. to get over
7. doing
8. to do
9. to live
10. to do
11. seeing
12. to visit
13. getting

EXERCISE 2

2. is tired of being
3. enjoys meeting
4. believes in talking
5. forgot to bring
6. remember telling
7. stopped to get
8. afford to lose
9. refuses to live
10. intends to make
11. agreed to help
12. offered to drive

EXERCISE 3

3. It's useful to work together.
4. Being careful is smart.
5. Being anxious all the time isn't good.
6. It isn't dangerous to fly.
7. It's a good idea to do relaxation exercises.
8. It's wonderful to travel.

EXERCISE 4

I want ~~reporting~~ *to report* on my progress. I'm very happy

that I finally stopped ~~to procrastinate~~ *procrastinating* and decided ~~doing~~ *to do*

something about my fear of flying. It was really getting

in the way of my professional and social life. ~~To join~~ *Joining*

this support group was one of the smartest decisions

I've ever made.

Last week, I had a business meeting in Texas. Instead

of ~~drive~~ *driving* all day to get there, I was able to ~~getting~~ *get* on a

plane and be there in just a few hours. What a

difference!

I remember ~~to work~~ *working* on an important project once,

and I actually had to drop out because it required a lot of

flying and I just couldn't do it. I was anxious all the time.

My fear was beginning to hurt my friendships, too. I

was dating a woman I liked a lot and we were supposed

to go on a trip. I canceled at the last minute because it

required ~~to take~~ *taking* a plane.

Now I'm looking forward to ~~do~~ *doing* a lot of traveling. I

know fear of flying is a universal problem, but it doesn't

have to be mine! It's a big world out there, and I plan

on ~~enjoy~~ *enjoying* it.

EXERCISE 5
Answers will vary.

PART 8 PRONOUNS AND PHRASAL VERBS
UNIT 27 Reflexive and Reciprocal Pronouns

EXERCISE 1

2. himself
3. itself
4. herself
5. yourself, yourselves OR
   yourselves, yourself
6. themselves
7. itself
8. ourselves

EXERCISE 2

2. each other
3. herself
4. themselves
5. each other's
6. herself
7. yourselves
8. itself
9. ourselves
10. each other

EXERCISE 3

2. one another OR each other
3. itself
4. each other OR one another
5. myself
6. yourselves
7. himself
8. ourselves
9. yourself
10. themselves

EXERCISE 4

2. are criticizing each other OR one another
3. is going to help himself
4. are talking to themselves
5. are introducing themselves
6. are talking to each other
7. drove herself
8. blames OR is blaming himself
9. are enjoying each other's OR one another's
10. are thanking each other OR one another

EXERCISE 5

I really enjoyed ~~me~~ *myself* at Gina's party! Hank was there,
and we talked to ~~ourselves~~ *each other* OR *one another* quite a bit. He's a little
depressed about losing his job. The job ~~himself~~ *itself* wasn't
that great, but the loss of income has really impacted
his life. He's disappointed in himself. He thinks it's all his
own fault, and he blames ~~him~~ *himself* for the whole thing.

Hank introduced ~~myself~~ *me* to several of his friends. I
spoke a lot to this one woman, Cara. We have a lot of
things in common, and after just an hour, we felt like
we had known ~~each other's~~ *each other* forever. Cara ~~himself~~ *herself* is a
computer programmer, just like me.

At first, I was nervous about going to the party
alone. I sometimes feel a little uncomfortable when
I'm in a social situation by ~~oneself~~ *myself*. But this time was
different. Before I went, I kept telling myself to relax.
My roommate too kept telling ~~myself~~ *me*, "Don't be so
hard on ~~you~~ *yourself*! Just have fun!" That's what I advised Hank
to do, too.

Before we left the party, Hank and I promised ~~us~~ *each other* OR *one another* OR *Ø* to
keep in touch. I hope to see him again soon.

EXERCISE 6

Answers will vary.

UNIT 28 Phrasal Verbs

EXERCISE 1

2. back
3. in
4. out
5. out
6. back
7. up
8. on
9. up

10. out
11. out
12. out
13. over
14. off
15. over
16. down
17. on
18. out

EXERCISE 2

2. Pick out, help . . . out
3. look up
4. Set up, talk over
5. Write up
6. Look . . . over
7. Do . . . over
8. Hand . . . in

EXERCISE 3

2. clean it up
3. call her back
4. turn it down
5. wake him up
6. turn it down
7. hand them in
8. drop it off

EXERCISE 4

2. Point out common mistakes. OR Point common mistakes out.
3. Talk them over.
4. Pick out a new problem. OR Pick a new problem out.
5. Work it out with the class.
6. Write up the results. OR Write the results up.
7. Go on to the next unit.
8. Make up the final exam questions. OR Make the final exam questions up.
9. Hand them out.
10. Set up study groups. OR Set study groups up.
11. Help them out.
12. Call off Friday's class. OR Call Friday's class off.

EXERCISE 5

How are things going? I'm already into the second
month of the spring semester, and I've got a lot of
work to do. For science class, I have to write a term
paper. The professor made ~~over~~ *up* a list of possible topics.
After looking ~~over them~~ *them over*, I think I've picked one out.
I'm going to write about chimpanzees and animal
intelligence. I've already looked_∧ *up* some information about
them online ~~up~~. I found ~~up~~ *out* some very interesting facts.

Did you know that their hands look very much like
their feet, and that they have fingernails and toenails?
Their thumbs and big toes are "opposable." This makes
it easy for them to pick things ~~out~~ *up* with both their
fingers and toes. Their arms are longer than their legs.
This helps ~~out them~~ *them out*, too, because they can reach fruit

growing on thin branches that would not otherwise support their weight. Adult males weigh between 90 and 115 pounds (40 and 52 kilograms), and they are about 4 feet (1.2 meters) high when they stand ~~out~~ *up*.

Like humans, chimpanzees are very social. They travel in groups called "communities." Mothers bring ~~out~~ *up* their chimps, who stay with them until about the age of seven. Even after the chimps grow up, there is still a lot of contact with other chimpanzees.

I could go on, but I need to stop writing now so I can clean ~~out~~ *up* my room (it's a mess!) a little before going to bed. It's late, and I have to get ~~early up~~ *up early* tomorrow morning for my 9:00 class.

Please let me know how you are. Or call me. I'm often out, but if you leave a message, I'll call ~~back you~~ *you back* as soon as I can. It would be great to speak to you.

EXERCISE 6

Answers will vary.

PART 9 MORE MODALS AND SIMILAR EXPRESSIONS
UNIT 29 Necessity: *Have (got) to, Must, Can't*

EXERCISE 1

2. must pass
3. must not forget
4. must obey
5. must stop
6. must not drive
7. must not change
8. must turn on
9. must not leave
10. must wear
11. must not talk
12. must sit
13. must . . . drink
14. must know

EXERCISE 2

2. don't have to be
3. have to drive
4. doesn't have to go
5. have to drive
6. have to wear
7. don't have to use
8. have to carry
9. don't have to have
10. have to keep
11. don't have to keep

EXERCISE 3

2. don't have to
3. don't have to
4. must not
5. don't have to
6. don't have to
7. must not
8. don't have to

EXERCISE 4

2. A: Do . . . have to stop
   B: Yes, we do.
3. A: have . . . had to use
4. A: Did . . . have to work
   B: No, I didn't.
5. B: 'll have to get OR 'm going to have to get
6. B: had to drive
7. B: did . . . have to pay
8. A: Has . . . had to pay
   B: No, he hasn't.
9. A: Will (OR Do) . . . have to get OR Am . . . going to have to get
   B: Yes, you will. OR Yes, you do. OR Yes, you are.
10. B: has to have
11. A: do . . . have to get

EXERCISE 5

2. You must stop.
3. You must not drive faster than 50 miles per hour.
4. You must not turn when the light is red.
5. You must not enter.
6. You can't pass another car.
7. You must drive in the direction of the arrow.
8. You can't drive 70 miles per hour.
9. You can't turn left.
10. You don't have to move your car at 6:00 p.m.

EXERCISE 6

Sorry I haven't written before, but there are so many things I've ~~must~~ *had to* do since we moved to California. For one, I have to ~~taking~~ *take* a driving test. My brother is lucky. He ~~must not~~ *doesn't have to* take one because he got a license when he was a student here. And you really have to drive if you live here—it's very hard to get around without a car! So, I've been studying the Driver Handbook, and I've found some pretty interesting—and sometimes strange—things:

• You can't smoke when a minor (that's someone under the age of eighteen) is in the car.
• You can use a cell phone, but you ~~has~~ *have* got to use one with a hands-free device.
• You must ~~no~~ *not* "dump or abandon animals on a highway." (I can't imagine anyone doing this, can you?) If you do, you will probably ~~must~~ *have to* pay a fine of $1,000, or go to jail for six months, or both!

have to
Did you ~~must~~ take a road test when you moved to Italy?
to
I've got_∧go now. Let me hear from you!

EXERCISE 7

Answers will vary.

UNIT 30 Expectations: *Be supposed to*

EXERCISE 1

2. is supposed to send
3. are supposed to provide
4. aren't supposed to provide
5. isn't supposed to pay for
6. is supposed to pay for
7. aren't supposed to pay for
8. is supposed to pay for
9. aren't supposed to give
10. are supposed to give
11. isn't supposed to supply
12. is supposed to pay for
13. is supposed to provide

EXERCISE 2

2. Item 2: She was supposed to write the month first. OR She wasn't supposed to write the day first.
3. Item 4: She was supposed to print (OR write) her last name. OR She wasn't supposed to print (OR write) her first name.
4. Item 5: She was supposed to print (OR write) her first name. OR She wasn't supposed to print (OR write) her last name.
5. Item 6: She was supposed to write (OR include) her zip code.
6. Item 7: She was supposed to write (OR include) her state and (her) zip code.
7. Item 8: She was supposed to sign her name. OR She wasn't supposed to print her name.
8. Item 9: She was supposed to write the date.

EXERCISE 3

1. is (OR was) supposed to land
2. are . . . supposed to get
3. Are . . . supposed to call
   Yes, we are.
4. are . . . supposed to tip
5. Is . . . supposed to be
   No, it isn't.
6. are . . . supposed to do
   're supposed to leave
7. Is . . . supposed to rain
   . . . it isn't.
8. Are . . . supposed to shake

EXERCISE 4

2. A: Adam wasn't supposed to become an engineer.
   B: He was supposed to be an architect.
3. A: Erica and Adam were supposed to get married in June.
   B: They weren't supposed to get married in September.
4. A: They weren't supposed to have a big wedding.
   B: They were supposed to have a small one.
5. A: They were supposed to have a short ceremony. OR The ceremony was supposed to be short.
   B: They weren't supposed to have a long ceremony. OR The ceremony wasn't supposed to be long.
6. A: They were supposed to go to London for their honeymoon.
   B: They weren't supposed to go to Bermuda.
7. A: They were supposed to live in Boston.
   B: They weren't supposed to live in Amherst.
8. A: They weren't supposed to rent an apartment.
   B: They were supposed to buy a house.

EXERCISE 5

Here we are in beautiful Bermuda. It's sunny, 80°F,
it's
and ~~it will~~ supposed to get even warmer later today.

I'm so glad we decided to come here for our
were
honeymoon. We ~~was~~ supposed to go to London, but
we decided we really needed a relaxing beach vacation
instead. The hotel is very nice. We were supposed to
get a standard double room, but when they found out
we were on our honeymoon, they upgraded us to a
suite with an ocean view. Tonight we're eating at Chez
It's supposed
Marcel's. ~~It supposes~~ to be one of the best restaurants
on the island.
I'm supposed
Gotta go now. ~~I suppose~~ to meet Adam in a few
He was
minutes. ~~He's~~ supposed to join me at the beach, but
decided to play some tennis instead.

Thanks for offering to pick us up at the airport.
arrive
We're supposed to ~~arriving~~ at 5:30 p.m., but check with
the airport before to see if there are any delays. See you
soon!

EXERCISE 6

Answers will vary.

UNIT 31 Future Possibility: *May, Might, Could*

EXERCISE 1

2. may go
3. could be
4. might be able to
5. might want
6. may not be
7. could go
8. might not understand
9. might not want
10. could stay
11. might be

EXERCISE 2

2. might buy
3. is going to rain
4. is going to see
5. might go
6. is going to work
7. might have
8. is going to call
9. is going to read
10. might write

EXERCISE 3

How are you? It's the Fourth of July, and it's raining
really hard. They say it could ~~cleared~~ *clear* up later. Then
again, it ~~could~~ *might* OR *may* not. You never know with the weather.

Do you remember my brother, Eric? He says hi. He
might ~~has~~ *have* dinner with me on Saturday night. We may go
to a new Mexican restaurant that just opened in the mall.
I definitely ~~might take~~ *am going to take* OR *am taking* some vacation time next
month. Perhaps we could do something together. It
might ~~not~~ be fun to do some traveling. What do you
think? Let me know.

EXERCISE 4

Answers will vary.

UNIT 32 Present Conclusions: *Must, Have (got) to, May, Might, Could, Can't*

EXERCISE 1

2. must not be
3. must feel
4. must not have
5. must know
6. must have
7. must not hear
8. must feel
9. must have
10. must not be
11. must speak
12. must not study
13. must have
14. must not eat
15. must be

EXERCISE 2

1. might
2. must
3. must
4. might, could
5. could, must
6. must, couldn't

EXERCISE 3

2. She must
3. They must
4. He must be
5. She might (not) OR may (not) OR could
6. It must be
7. It must be
8. They might be OR may be OR could be
9. She must
10. He might be OR may be OR could be
11. They must be

EXERCISE 4

2. Could
3. can't
4. Bob
5. Chet
6. could
7. might
8. Dave
9. could
10. couldn't
11. Allen

EXERCISE 5

Just got home. It's really cold outside. The
temperature ~~could~~ *must* be below freezing because the
walkway is all covered with ice. What a day! We went
down to the police station to look at photos. I was
amazed. They must ~~having~~ *have* hundreds of photos. They
kept showing us more and more. We kept looking, but it
was difficult to be sure. After all, we only saw the burglar
for a few seconds. They've got to have other witnesses
besides us! There were a lot of people at the mall that
day. We ~~may not~~ *can't* OR *couldn't* be the only ones who got a look at the
burglar! That's the one thing I'm certain of! In spite of
our uncertainty with the photos, the detective was very
patient. I guess he must be used to witnesses like us.
Nevertheless, it ~~have~~ *has* to be frustrating for him. I know
the police ~~may~~ *must* really want to catch this guy!

EXERCISE 6

Answers will vary.